# A GENTLE CYNIC

# THE WORDS OF KOHELETH
### IN THEIR ORIGINAL FORM, STRIPPED OF SUBSEQUENT INTERPOLATIONS, MAXIMS AND COMMENTS

# A Gentle Cynic

## BEING A TRANSLATION
## OF THE
# BOOK OF KOHELETH
### COMMONLY KNOWN AS ECCLESIASTES
### STRIPPED OF LATER ADDITIONS

#### ALSO

## ITS ORIGIN, GROWTH AND
## INTERPRETATION

BY

## MORRIS JASTROW, JR., PH.D., LL.D
PROFESSOR IN THE UNIVERSITY OF PENNSYLVANIA

"Come, fill the Cup and in the fire of Spring
Your Winter-garment of Repentance fling;
The Bird of Time has but a little way
To flutter—and the Bird is on the Wing."
OMAR KHAYYAM

## PHILADELPHIA & LONDON
## J. B. LIPPINCOTT COMPANY
### 1919

PRINTED BY J. B. LIPPINCOTT COMPANY
AT THE WASHINGTON SQUARE PRESS
PHILADELPHIA, U. S. A.

TO

GEORGE AARON BARTON
*BRYN MAWR COLLEGE*

ALBERT TOBIAS CLAY
*YALE UNIVERSITY*

AND

JAMES ALAN MONTGOMERY
*UNIVERSITY OF PENNSYLVANIA*

# FOREWORD

HIS work is an endeavor to place before a general public, and in popular form, the results of the critical study of the Old Testament as applied to a single book in the collection. I have chosen the book commonly known as Ecclesiastes, because of the intensely human interest attaching to this specimen of the ancient literature of Palestine.

The designation "Ecclesiastes", to be taken in the sense of one who addresses an Ecclesia *i.e.*, an assembly, is an attempt on the part of the Greek translator of the book to render the Hebrew word Koheleth (pronounced Ko-háy-leth), which is the name assumed by the author of the book, and the underlying stem of which means to "assemble." Since the author, however, wanted us to regard Koheleth as a proper name, why translate it at all? Ecclesiastes is a harsh and forbidding title for a book that is marked by a singular lightness of touch, and I have therefore retained throughout this work the name Koheleth for the book, and have chosen "A Gentle Cynic" as an appropriate designation to describe both the character of the book and the author, who has concealed his personality behind a *nom de plume*. [1]

[1] See p. 65.

The book is not only intensely human, it is also remarkably modern in its spirit. Koheleth belongs to the small coterie of books that do not grow old. It does not follow that such books are to be placed among the great classics of world literature, though in some instances they do enjoy this distinction, as in the case of the Book of Job and the Quatrains of Omar Khayyam, which are likewise remarkably modern. Nor is the reverse proposition true that all the great classics have a modern flavor. The spirit of Homer is that of antiquity, whereas that of Horace is modern. Molière is intensely human, but because he reflects so exclusively the foibles of his days, he does not make the strong appeal to the modern world as does Shakespeare, who is human *and* modern. Of two authors who are contemporaneous, one may remain modern and the other not, though both may be reckoned among the great. Witness Goethe and Schiller, the former speaking to the present age in a way that the latter does not.

Koheleth is modern, because with great literary skill he deals with those aspects of human life which are always the same. He is almost brutally frank in holding the mirror up to life. For all that, he is neither a scoffer nor a pessimist. He loves life and has intense sympathy with the struggles and sufferings of humanity, but he smiles at the attempts of zealous reformers to change human nature or to improve a state of things, which (as he believes) follows logically from the conditions under which

8

mankind carves out its career. Koheleth is not a cold and severely logical philosopher, intent upon building up a system of thought, but an easy-going dilettante who unfolds in a series of charming, witty and loosely connected *causeries* his view of life, as gained by a long and varied experience.

The defects of his attitude towards life are so apparent that they need hardly be pointed out. He does not pose as a guide to be followed, nor does he help us in solving the problems of life. He would be willing to confess that he has no solution, because —and this is perhaps his chief defect—he sees no *aim* in life, no goal towards which mankind is tending. Koheleth is serious in what he says, though he always speaks with a slight ironical smile on his lips, but he does not want us to take him *too* seriously, just as he himself does not want to take life too seriously. The human interest of the book is all the more intense because of its main conclusion, that life itself is a paradox. Life is made to be enjoyed, and yet enjoyment is "vanity."

It is a strange book to have slipped into a sacred collection. This would never have happened had the book been permitted to remain in the form which the author originally gave it. Instead of taking Koheleth as he was, the attempt was made by those who did not approve of his tone and of his attitude to twist his thought to conform to the conventional views and beliefs of the age. How this was done will be set forth in detail, in order to justify my new rendering and to clear up the various questions raised by the book. The bearings of the modifications to which the original book of Koheleth was subjected on its character as a sacred book will also be considered.

For the book in its present form is the result of manipulation at various hands that have made additions to it in the form of comments, insertions and counter arguments with a two-fold purpose in view, to make the utterances in the book conform to the tradition of Solomon, to whom an uncritical age ascribed the authorship, and to make the teachings more palatable to the pious and conservative, who were to read it as part of a sacred collection. The result has been to produce an entirely different book from the one which the author intended. It is this modified Koheleth—practically a second Koheleth by the side of the first one—that has found a place in the sacred collection. If we wish to get back to the *real* Koheleth, we must lop off all additions made to it, which additions constitute over one-fourth of the present book. This I have done in the translation, with an indication at each point of the extraneous material and an explanation of its character and purpose.

The thought of the book as it stands in our Bible translations cannot possibly be clear to the general reader. Those who manipulated the text of the original Koheleth in order to convert an unorthodox production into an unobjectionable one succeeded in their aim, but at the cost of introducing contradictions and inconsistencies of which this new Koheleth is full. If we can imagine Homer or Virgil published with the scholia of later commentators put into the *body* of the text, or the Quatrains of Omar Khayyam with the comments and pious reflections of orthodox Mohammedans added, as though forming *part* of the original, in order to counteract unorthodox sentiments about "wine, woman and song," one will be able to form an impression of the text as finally fixed and as it now stands in our Bible. At the same time, while recognizing what commentators in the interests of orthodoxy have made of Koheleth, we must not fall into the error of charging such commentators with any intention to practice a wilful deceit. We must always bear in mind that every production in an age which had not as yet developed the sense of individual authorship was subject to constant modification. Such modification was in part an index of the interest that a new production had aroused. An ancient book never received a *final* form, so long as its message retained its vitality. The modifications which a piece of writing underwent might be made by those who agreed with it, or by those who were not in sympathy with it. The manipulators of Koheleth were opposed to its tone and thought, but they were not conscious of any wrong in furnishing through additions their *answers* to Koheleth's arguments and conclusions, any more

than a modern editor in republishing some philosophical or theological treatise would be conscious of guilt in adding notes to controvert the
position taken by the author whom he is rein-
troducing to the public. The separation of an
editor's observations from the *body* of the text,
as against an incorporation of comments and
super-comments *in* the text is just the difference
between literary production in an age in which
authorship is anonymous or collective, and one
in which authorship has become personal and
distinctive.

In my restoration of the original text on the
basis of my own researches, I have also availed
myself of the work of the many scholars, who have
during the past century devoted themselves to
the study of the book with the application of the
critical and historical method that has now become
the universally recognized *conditio sine quâ non*
for an intelligent appreciation of both the Old and
the New Testament. Those who are interested in
questions of technical detail, may be referred to
Professor George A. Barton's "Critical and Exegetical Commentary on the Book of Ecclesiastes"
(New York, 1908), and to A. H. McNeile's "Intro-
.duction to Ecclesiastes" (Cambridge, 1904), two
excellent and comprehensive works.

I should like also to mention especially the
valuable textual and critical notes to Koheleth by
Arnold B. Ehrlich, many of whose corrections and
interpretations I have adopted. These notes will

be found in a monumental work, indispensable to the specialist, under the title "Randglossen zur Hebräischen Bibel" (Leipzig, 1908-14), in seven volumes, covering all the books of the Old Testament and embodying the results of a life-long study of the Bible by this remarkably keen scholar. My own book being intended for the general reader, I have avoided technical discussions and unnecessary references.

With those who are still able to approach the Bible with a naïve faith in its literal inspiration I have no quarrel, but for those who are unable to do so—and they constitute the bulk of the educated public—the books of the Bible need to be reinterpreted in the light of modern researches, which, it should be made clear affect our beliefs *about* the Bible, but not belief *in* the Bible. The primary motive which impels me to make the effort to so reinterpret one of the most striking and one of the most charming books in the collection is the desire to make a contribution—however modest—towards securing for the general public the *positive* gains of the new epoch for Biblical studies which set in with the discovery, made by a French physician, Jean Astruc,[2] that the Pentateuch, until then accepted by tradition as the work in *toto* of one author—Moses—consisted of several documents, each of independent origin, which had been pieced together. The discovery seemed quite inno-

---

[2] The title of Astruc's work is "Conjectures sur les mémoires originaux dont il paraît que Moyse s'est servi pour composer le livre de la Genèse." (Brussels, 1753.)

13

cent on the surface, particularly as Astruc made
the concession to a time-honored belief by still
assuming Moses to have been the one who welded
the documents into a literary unity.  But the
change from Moses as the one to whom the entire
Pentateuch had been revealed, to Moses as a mere
compiler of documents that had been produced by
others—and by human hands at that—aimed a
blow at tradition, the fatal character of which
could not be concealed by any appearance of com-
promise.

*C'est le premier pas qui coûte.*  A new method
of approach to the study of the sacred collection
had been inaugurated.  This method, modified and
perfected by successive generations of scholars,
chiefly in Germany, France, Holland and England
and applied to all the books of the Old and New
Testament, led inevitably to the substitution of
historical criticism in place of a naïve and uncritical
tradition that had in the course of time grown up
around the Bible.  The result has been to give
a historical setting to the unfolding of religious
thought among the Hebrews from primitive beliefs which at one time they shared with their
fellow Semites, to the advanced conception of a
spiritual Power of universal scope as the single
source of all phenomena in nature and as controling the destinies of the human race.  In keeping
with this, the religious, social and political institu-
tions of the Hebrews have been shown to follow
an order of development that carried us still fur-

# FOREWORD

ther from the traditional view of the course taken by Hebrew history. The religious movement inaugurated by the prophets of the ninth century and culminating in Judaism has been placed by the critical method in its proper light. We can now trace the religion of the Hebrews from the circumscribed Yahwism of the Mosaic age to the ethical monotheism of the post-exilic period, which begins at the close of the sixth century B.C.

But this historical and critical method has in turn entailed a complete recasting of our views as to the origin, date and method of composition of the books of the Old and the New Testament. So thoroughly has this work been done that at the present time the results of the critical study of the Old Testament[3] are accepted by all scholars who are willing to apply to a sacred collection the same method that holds good for secular literature. The storm which raged several decades ago over the "Higher Criticism" has subsided, though occasionally distant echoes of thunder can still be heard, and faint streaks of lightning still flash from pulpits and from the halls of religious conventions. The general public also knows of these results and either is indifferent to them or accepts them with the realization that this acceptance does not involve hostility to religious faith, as is stupidly maintained by those who denounce the "critics" without understanding them. For all that, in

[3] For an admirable and brief survey of the results of the modern critical method, the reader is referred to Professor G. B. Gray's "Critical Introduction to the O. T." (London, 1913.)

popular writings and even in learned works, unless the author happens to be a specialist in Oriental scholarship, the positive gains of the new method find scant recognition. When Hebrew history is referred to, the traditional view is just as apt to be brought forward as the new setting for that history, secured through the labors of modern scholars. Biblical characters are referred to in popular writings with little attempt to distinguish between creations of myth, folk-lore or priestly tradition like Samson, Isaac and Aaron, and genuine historical personages like Moses, Gideon, Samuel and Saul; and in the case of such historical personages, probable facts are not separated from legendary accretions. The Pentateuch is still commonly spoken of in pulpits as though it dated from the days of Moses. Psalms are still commonly associated with David, though the Psalms represent the Hymn Book of the Jewish community in the post-exilic days, and Proverbs, Song of Songs and Ecclesiastes are ascribed to Solomon, though none of these works originated till many centuries after the death of the monarch who was himself idealized—as was also David—by legend and tradition into a figure bearing only a slight relation to the *real* Solomon.

Now all this would perhaps be of minor consideration if it did not actually prevent an intelligent approach to the books of the Old and the New Testament on the part of those who can no longer read the Bible with that simple faith in the tradition *that grew up* around the Bible, and that protected their great-grandfathers and great-grandmothers from seeing the difficulties which the modern reader encounters. From whatever point of view we regard the Bible—whether from the angle of religion or of literature or of history—the collection is too valuable to be exposed to the risk of being either lost or misunderstood; and unless the books of the Bible are understood, they are practically lost to readers imbued with the modern spirit.

In presenting Koheleth in a new garb, *minus* the trimmings which were attached to the original composition, it is my hope to make a remarkable literary production more intelligible than is possible by reading it in any of our present-day translations of the Old Testament, which are all modeled on the classic "authorized" version of 1611, and which all assume the book to be a literary *unit* in its present form. In other words, I have tried to give the reader the book of Koheleth in its original form, as nearly as that is at present possible; and it is only fair to add that, in order to do so, it has been necessary to correct the text in places where in the course of being copied by one scribe after the other it has manifestly become corrupt. The total number of such corrections, however, is not excessively large.

In the translation, I have disregarded the ordinary division into chapters which is very late and not found in ancient manuscripts of Biblical

books, and, instead, have divided the "Words of Koheleth," as the attached title reads, into twenty-four sections, each dealing with some phase of the general problem with which the author is concerned. For the sake of convenience, I have added on the margin the corresponding chapter and verses in our ordinary Bibles, so that those who so desire may compare my rendering with the "authorized" version and its successors. I have felt entirely free to choose my own wording, with no sense of being bound by the "authorized" version, which as a classic of English literature will, of course, always retain its place, but which, as a *translation* of a text better understood after a lapse of three hundred years, can be improved upon on almost every page. Where I deviate in more than a mere choice of words from the generally accepted rendering of a passage, I have tried to justify my view in the brief notes attached to the translation. Slight and obviously necessary textual changes I have passed over in silence; more radical ones I have briefly commented on in the notes. These notes are not in any sense technical, and have therefore been made as brief and as simple as possible, just enough to enable the reader to follow the interpretation of the book according to my understanding of it. All the additions to the text will also be found in these notes; and for further convenience I have grouped all the additions in the Appendix under three divisions. In this way the reader, with the further assistance of the discussion preceding the translation, will be able to see for himself just how the book was manipulated, the nature and purpose of the additions made, how its original thought was obscured or given a different turn, and how it gradually grew until it received the shape that it has in the usual translations of the Bible.

I feel that no apology is needed for the length of this discussion, which is, as already suggested, an attempt to give to the general public some of the positive gains of the critical study of the Old Testament, as carried on by many scholars in many lands during the past century. The recognition of these gains will, I firmly believe, help to remove the misunderstandings still current regarding the nature and purpose of the historical, literary and critical study of the Bible. I beg to call special attention to the sections[4] in which I have discussed some of the aspects of the relation of criticism to tradition, and where I have tried to show that in rejecting traditional views about the Biblical books —affecting their origin, date and manner of composition—there is more than a compensating gain in bringing us nearer to an intelligent appreciation of the contents of these books and—I venture to add—of their real value. The religious truths embodied in the Biblical books are independent of questions of text, origin and composition, with which alone historical and literary criticism is concerned.

---

[4] XIII to XVI.

Those who take the trouble of reading the results of my investigations will, I venture to think, find all the other important questions raised by the book, its thought and its aim, and its relationship to the beliefs of the age in which it was written, to Greek ideas and to Jewish orthodoxy, fully covered, and in such a way as to illuminate the "Words of Koheleth" as a human document. In order to understand an ancient book, we must make the attempt to get a picture in our minds of the time and the conditions under which it was written. That aim has been before me above all else, and I shall be happy if I shall have succeeded in making Koheleth a *living* book to the modern reader. It is my hope and intention to treat in the same way two other Biblical books, the Book of Job and the Song of Songs, which, like Koheleth, need to be reinterpreted, by means of a utilization of the results of a critical study of them, in order that they may make their appeal to our age.

In committing my interpretation of the "Gentle Cynic" to the tender mercies of (I hope) an equally gentle reader, I feel assured that he will become as fondly attached to Koheleth—even though, perhaps, not approving of all his teachings and utterances—as I have grown. It remains for me to express my obligations, as in the case of all my writings, to my wife for the help received from her in the form of suggested improvements in the presentation of my results and in the translation itself. She has also, as usual, read a proof. To her

# FOREWORD

direct aid as well as to her sympathy with all my work and to her encouragement to carry it on, I owe any merits that I may have achieved in the course of my life. It is both a pleasure and a privilege to combine on the dedication page the names of three dear colleagues who are associated in my mind together, to whose firm friendship and stimulating companionship, I owe much—very much.

MORRIS JASTROW, Jr.

University of Pennsylvania
January, 1919

# CONTENTS

# CONTENTS

# A GENTLE CYNIC

## THE ORIGIN, GROWTH AND INTERPRETATION OF THE WORDS OF KOHELETH

# A Gentle Cynic

## I

## A STRANGE BOOK IN A SACRED CANON

T the close of the Book of Koheleth some reader or commentator has added the warning, "Beware, my son, of the writing of many books without end," as though to caution us against taking too seriously the teachings of a book, which seemed dangerous from the point of view of conventional morality. The warning sounds a challenge to every writer to justify himself in adding another to the more than three million books that have been produced since the literary impulse—Koheleth would call it "a sorry business"—first seized hold of man on this little planet of ours. Koheleth himself would, no doubt, echo the suggestion contained in the warning that books follow one another in endless succession, because it is a part of the "nature of the beast." Man writes because he cannot help it. The point is not *what* man writes, but *that* he writes and that he goes on writing as naturally as he goes on living, though Koheleth well knows that both man's life and his book will come to an end.

There is no *final* book on any subject—no

last word. Why, then, add another to share the fate of gathering dust on the shelves of libraries or of being ground to pulp to form the material for some successor? Why write if a book is to be produced, only to be offered up as a sacrifice to bring into existence the next one, a process which gives to bookmaking some of the aspects of cannibalism? But the warning against the making of endless books comes with special force, if the book in question is to be a new translation of an ancient one. Why present a book written over 2100 years ago, in a new garb? Is not Koheleth included in every translation of the Old Testament that has appeared since the days of Wycliffe and Luther? Are there not enough commentaries on this book in every modern language?[5] The justification is to be found in the fact that Koheleth was admitted by a strange fate into a collection of sacred writings. The author had been dead for several centuries before his production was thus canonized, or he would first have smiled at finding himself in company with prophets and psalmists, and then after a closer inspection, upon seeing how his work had been altered in order to adapt it to a group to which it did not belong, he might have grown indignant. At all events, he would have had difficulty in recognizing his offspring.

---

[5] A long list of commentaries and monographs on Ecclesiastes will be found in Professor G. A. Barton's "Critical and Exegetical Commentary" on the "Book of Ecclesiastes" (N. Y., 1908) pp. 18-31, in McNeile's "Introduction to Ecclesiastes" (Cambridge, 1904) p. 55, and in Ludwig Levy's "Das Buch Qoheleth" (Leipzig, 1912) pp. 65-67.

The privilege of being included in a sacred collection turned out to be a misfortune for the book, for it led to its being totally misunderstood, or, rather, intentionally modified so as to conceal its real purport. Koheleth is in reality, as we shall see, a most unorthodox production. Its teachings run counter to the conventional beliefs of the times in which it was composed. It offended the pious by its bold skepticism and displeased those who believed in a Creator who stamped his handiwork with the verdict "And behold it was good," by its undisguised, albeit gentle cynicism. Critical scholarship, as the result of the combined activity of many scholars of many lands during the past century, now recognizes that the book, as it stands in our Bible, consists of a kernel to which liberal additions have been made. These additions which were introduced, as we shall see, for the express purpose of counteracting the effect of Koheleth's unconventional views and to give a more orthodox turn to his thought are to be found in each one of the twelve chapters into which the book was arbitrarily divided.[6]  In some chapters, the additions consist merely of a phrase or of a sentence skillfully inserted here and there at a critical point in the discussion; in others, as in the eighth chapter, the additions are almost equal to the original sec-

---

[6] It must be borne in mind that the division into chapters in our Bible is late and does not occur in ancient manuscripts of the Hebrew text. In my translation (see the foreword, page 17), I have discarded these divisions, and instead have divided the book into 24 sections, each one dealing with some aspect of the general theme.

tion, while again in some, as in the seventh and tenth chapters, the supplementary material is in excess of the original portion of the chapter.[7] Besides these conspicuous additions, amounting in all to more than one-fourth of the book, there are little glosses and comments of a miscellaneous character, likewise interspersed throughout, which correspond to our foot-notes to a text. Now it is manifestly impossible to obtain a view of what the book was in its original form, unless in a translation we lop off all additions and insertions, as well as the glosses and little comments. To translate the book as it stands, as has hitherto been done, precludes the possibility of grasping the character that the author intended to give to his production.

The acceptance of Koheleth into the Canon was a gradual process. We know that as late as the first century before this era it was not generally regarded as on a par with the books of the collection of ancient Hebrew literature, which had to be handled with special reverence. Even then it would never have been admitted among sacred writings by the council of learned and pious Jews, who at Jamnia in Palestine fixed the Canon at the end of the first century of our era, had it not been for the additions which toned down the skeptical tenor of its teachings and controverted its bold defiance of accepted beliefs. The circumstance that the authorship was attributed to Solomon was a

---

[7] See for details below pp. 71-86, and in the comments to the translations.

vital factor in leading to its inclusion in the Canon, but even this would not have secured its admission without the additions which constitute such a considerable part of the work in its present form, and which made it practically a different kind of a book. The question arises, how were these additions made, or, rather, first of all, how was it possible for anyone to conceive of making them?

## II

### BEFORE THE DAYS OF "AUTHORSHIP"

To us who are accustomed to think of a book as the work of a single individual, brought out with the seal of authenticity attached to it under the name of its author, it must indeed seem strange that the original form of a piece of writing should be altered by subsequent additions; but authorship in the modern sense was unknown in antiquity until we reach the flourishing period of Greek literature. Up to that time, authorship was largely anonymous. A book might pass through many hands before receiving its final form; and in this form, two features which we naturally associate with a book, an author and a title, are conspicuous by their absence. Book writing was in the literal sense of the word *com-position*, that is, a putting together of documents which might date from various periods. A book involved a process of compilation in which various persons might take part. As a consequence, we have collective instead of individual authorship. A writer in the days of anonymous authorship laid no claim to special ownership to what he wrote—could lay no such claim. Everyone who could do so felt free to add to a manuscript that came into his hands. The person who wrote was of minor significance as against what he wrote, and if a piece of writing became popular by being circulated within a certain circle, it was destined to continual enlargement and modification. Indeed, this steady modification was an index of the popularity of a book. A book that had become definite in its form and that was no longer subject to change, was a *dead* book. The living book, which conveyed a message of real import to those who became acquainted with it, was one which had not yet become static. What we should regard as taking an unwarranted liberty with an author by changing what he had written, was from the ancient point of view not only perfectly legitimate but a real compliment to a book, an indication that it was a breathing organism and not a lifeless corpse. A book, moreover, continued to grow as long as it aroused sufficient interest to be added to and to be otherwise modified. From the modern point of view, a book is finished when the author puts his *finis* to it. The finished book begins its life—short or long—when it is issued from the press. From the ancient point of view the publication of a book in its final and definite form spelled its death—the end of the era which led to its production.

As for a title, in the days when writing was merely com-position, there was no occasion to give a name to a production which, as essentially a compilation, lacked any individualistic character. A title goes with individual authorship. A writer, having a definite subject in mind, will hit upon the idea, after having developed his subject systematically from beginning to end, of giving his production a name, just as an artist will be led to label a picture representing the execution of a plan formed and carried out; but when there is no author in this sense, no single individual who plans a book as a whole and gives it its final shape, there is no unity to a literary work thus produced. Hence in ancient days books had no title, because they lacked the unity which would suggest the desirability of giving to a literary product a distinctive designation. In Babylonia and Assyria, for example, where books were written on clay tablets, the tablets were numbered in succession and distinguished merely as "Tablet 1," "Tablet 2," etc., of a series described by the word or phrase with which the first tablet began. As a trace of this ancient custom, Papal Bulls are still known from the opening words of the document. Similarly, in the first division of the Old Testament, consisting of the five books forming the Pentateuch, the individual books have in Hebrew no title and are merely described by the opening word. So, for example, Genesis, which is the Greek translation of the Hebrew *Bereshith*, "Beginning," with which the book opens. In English usage we call the second book of the Pentateuch, "Exodus" which *is* a title descriptive of the contents of the book, but this title was given to it by the Greek translator. In Hebrew the book is designated as *Shemoth*, meaning "Names," which happens to be the opening word of the book.[8] The remaining three books are likewise known in Hebrew merely by the opening word; and even a book like Lamentations, written in the Post-Exilic period, is in Hebrew designated as *Echah*, meaning "Alas!", because it begins with that word.

If in the Hebrew text other books of the Old Testament, as the historical ones belonging to the second division, Judges, Kings, and Samuel, bear distinctive names, and if names like Psalms and Proverbs in the third division describe the contents of these books, it is because such designations are a reflex of the later period when the idea of authorship was beginning to make its way into the life of the Hebrews. With this advance comes the thought of giving a more definite designation to a literary production.

In the early period, however, the author was a negligible quantity, and necessarily so in an age which had not yet developed a sense of personal proprietorship in the written word. What a man *said* at that early period had far greater import and authority than what he *wrote*. Verbal utterances were scrupulously handed down in ancient times by oral tradition. The decisions of a judge,

---

[8] Strictly speaking it is the second word, the first being the demonstrative particle "These," which was not distinctive enough to serve as a designation.

the declarations of a political or military leader, the instructions of a teacher, the warnings of a prophet, the prayers of a religious poet, were transmitted by word of mouth with punctilious regard to their authenticity, but when an individual sank to the grade of a *mere* writer, his product became common property to be bandied about freely and without any concern for the vanity of the author who, in fact, was not recognized as having any prerogatives at all. A book was not a man's child to be guarded and petted by him as his very own, but a stray waif belonging to no one in particular. All ancient languages have a word (or several terms) for speaker, orator, teacher, but many have no distinctive expression, corresponding to our term "author." In Hebrew *e.g.* there is no such term; there is merely a word for writer (*sōfer*), and the writer is primarily a scribe. The *sōfer* writes, but whether what he writes is a copy from some model or something dictated to him, or some composition of his own is immaterial. He is merely a medium and no more important than the stylus with which he writes, or the clay, skin or leaf upon which he writes.

Authorship under these circumstances was necessarily and logically anonymous; and it is not accidental that the most ancient literary productions in all lands have come down to us without the authentic preservation of the names of their authors. The entire Babylonian literature is anonymous. There are plenty of names of copyists and scribes mentioned on the clay tablets, but no author; and if in Egyptian literature we occasionally come across the name of a person who writes an account of his travels, it is due to the accidental personal form which what he writes takes on. No one would think of him for that reason as an author. The hymns of the Rig Veda—the oldest of the literary productions of India—are all anonymous. Folk tales and folk songs, incantations, as well as prayers and hymns forming part of a ritual were in ancient times always anonymous. Even long after authorship had been definitely established as a factor in the literary life of a people, aye centuries thereafter, collections of fables and the entire field of story-telling in the East—witness the Arabian Nights—were anonymous productions.

In Western literature the Miracle and Morality plays are instances of collective and anonymous authorship, surviving to the Middle Ages and beyond. The "Passion Play" of Oberammergau, which still has the power to attract tens of thousands from all parts of the world whenever it is produced in the charming Tyrolean surroundings, falls in the same category. It has no author and belongs to the age of "collective" literary production, as do the various "Kasperl" plays which in the form of "Punch and Judy" shows still amuse the children of the present age. The drama, in fact, as late as the days of Shakespeare had not entirely emerged from this period of collective authorship; for Shakespeare begins his career by reshaping old plays to which his name becomes attached, although he is not in any individualistic sense their author, and it is impossible even for specialists in the study of the great dramatist to differentiate with certainty the older portions of such a play as, for example, "King Henry VI" and the parts which are due to Shakespeare. One is tempted to suggest that the persistence of the "tradition" of collective authorship in the drama may be a factor in accounting for the strange phenomenon that in the case of Shakespeare, living in the full daylight of history, a doubt as to the authenticity of his productions should have arisen— absurd though both the theories and the methods of the "Baconians" are.

As a survival of past conditions we have even in our days a good deal of anonymous authorship or, as we might also put it, collective authorship. Every proverb must have originated with some individual, but except in the case of quotations from some published work, collections of proverbs pass down the ages as anonymous. A modern newspaper furnishes a good illustration of the manner of book-making in antiquity. It is the work of many hands and it is issued anonymously. Editors and managers are not the authors, but merely the mediums of publication, just like the ancient scribes. The reporter when he puts his items into shape sinks his personality into the general anonymity that marks a newspaper; his work is modified by the city editor, precisely as a production in ancient times underwent modification by other hands than the one which gave it its original form. Even writers of editorials, in which it might be supposed the personal touch was essential, consciously or unconsciously fall into the general tone adopted by the newspaper in question, so that after the lapse of some time the members of an editorial board are unable to differentiate between one another's productions.[9] An almanac is another form of anonymous authorship, which furnishes perhaps a still closer analogy to the ancient method of book writing, so largely a matter of compilation and so essentially a gradual growth.

Among the Greeks who may be said to have invented the idea of authorship, literary production was at first likewise anonymous and non-individualistic. The Homeric poems are the work of many hands. Their composition is a gradual growth, and even if it be admitted that their final shape was due to the genius of a Greek rhapsodist who stood out preëminent among his fellows and whose name was Homer, that would not yet constitute Homer the author in the same sense in which Sophocles, Æschylus and Euripides are the authors of the plays that pass under their names. In the case of the Homeric poems, the personality (if there was one) is sunk in the work, whereas in the case of the dramatists of Greece, the production is dominated by the personality of the

---

[9] I have this on the authority of my friend Dr. Talcott Williams.

author. At all events, the Greeks appear to have been the first among the peoples of antiquity to have brought the author into the foreground. The Greeks created the author. In accord with the pronounced spirit of individualism, which is one of the distinguishing marks of Greek culture that manifests itself in art as well as in literature, the Greeks passed from anonymity in literary production to individualistic authorship. When we reach the golden period of Greek literature, an author's work is indelibly stamped with his personality. The result is a more marked differentiation between the productions of various authors, and this is particularly striking when we find the same theme treated by different authors, as in the case of the Œdipus story, which engages the genius of both Sophocles and Æschylus. The author becomes a figure of growing importance in public life, and from the domain of literature this importance is extended to the field of philosophical thought and physical science. Moreover, the written word comes to be viewed with the same reverence that was always attached to the spoken one. Oral tradition is supplemented by an increasing regard for written tradition until the latter comes to be looked upon as more authentic than the former; and since this depends upon the accuracy with which the productions of an author are transmitted through copyists, we have, instead of the former liberties taken with a literary product, growing punctiliousness to preserve a text in the form which the author gave it. The book becomes indissolubly associated with the author. So important does the author become that books which have come down anonymously are ascribed to authors by a tradition or by an inference that generally turns out to be untrustworthy. Instead of anonymity we now have pseudepigraphy, that is, trading on the name of an author in order to secure for a production the weight of his authority.

Whether in running this gamut from the extreme of utter indifference to authorship to the exaltation of the author to the point of borrowing or stealing his name to secure recognition for a literary work, is a gain—is another question. It no doubt stimulated literary production by holding out popularity and fame as an attractive bait, as well as pecuniary rewards for the successful author, but it also promoted the vanity which goes with authorship. It aroused the temptation to court popularity even at the cost of sincerity, and led to writing for writing's sake, creating precisely the evil "of writing many books without end" against which the commentator to Koheleth warns us. The ancient writer who could lay no claim to proprietorship in his productions wrote because he had something to say; the author whose career is bound up with literary production lives under the temptation of writing because he wishes to be known as saying something. The warnings against books without end suggests that the seriousness of writing diminishes in proportion to the amount. The ready writer may become the voluminous writer, and as our commentator adds "much discussion is a weariness of the flesh." If Koheleth wrote just for the pleasure of writing, the caution not to take him too seriously, with the implication that "the writing of many books without end" is to be added to the list of human vanities, is decidedly in place.

We in our days of overwhelming literary production, over and above the more than 100,000 newspapers that are printed daily throughout the world, are tempted to make such a fetish of the written word that we regard something as more apt to be true because we have seen it in print. As a matter of fact, written lies far outnumber spoken untruths. It is a far simpler matter to print a wrong statement than to make one verbally. Writing cannot be said to have increased mankind's regard for the truth. Literature is not an ethical force comparable to the influence exerted by the spoken word. The greatest figures in history, the world's greatest teachers as Moses, Buddha, Jesus and Mohammed did not write, as little as did the great generals (with some exceptions like Cæsar), and yet they shaped the course of human events to a far larger extent than writers have ever done.

Perhaps the most distinctive achievement of authorship will some day be recognized to be the creation of a new punctuation mark— the quotation sign—and a new crime—plagiarism. In the days of anonymous writing, plagiarism belongs to the virtues. It was an endorsement of a writer to use what he had written, an indication that his production had vitality, and was capable of being modified and elaborated, but woe to him who in the period of authorship fails to make acknowledgement for anything, be it merely an expressive phrase which he owes to a fellow craftsman. He is hurled into obloquy and assigned to a special purgatory. The author, however great his merits otherwise may be, is shorn of his reputation if he touches so much as a hair of the child that represents the mental offspring of a colleague.

## III

## BEGINNINGS OF LITERARY COMPILATION AMONG THE HEBREWS

This apparent digression has direct bearings on the strange fate that the Book of Koheleth encountered after it had been written by some unknown philosopher who lived in Palestine about the close of the third century before our era, and who aimed to set before us his attitude towards life, gained as a result of wide and varied experiences.

The period of the Babylonian Exile which set in with the capture and destruction of Jerusalem in 586 B.C. through the Babylonian ruler Nebuchadnezzar II. marks a turning-point in the literary history of the Hebrews, as well as in their political life and their religious development. Up to that time what literary production there was continued to be anonymous. The written word had not yet acquired the significance attaching to the spoken one. The popular traditions regarding the beginnings of things had been collected, as well as the folk-tales recounting the early experiences of the tribes and the adventures of the heroes and striking figures of the past. These collections in written form, but without authorship, existed in at least two forms, (1) a series of documents that originated in the Southern Hebrew Kingdom,[10] known from the preference for the name Yahweh as the designation of the national deity as the Yahwist documents, (2) the other series produced in the northern kingdom and known as the Elohist documents, because of the use of the more general designation Elohim, equivalent to our term "God" or Deity, in place of Yahweh, which is a specific name like Zeus or Thor. Several codes for the regulation of the government and of the ritual had been compiled, representing enlargements of the simple legislation in the form of oral decisions, that may be traced back to the beginnings of the national life of the Hebrews under a great leader whom tradition called Moses. These codes like the Yahwist and Elohist documents were anonymous, as were likewise the brief annals interspersed with the more detailed exploits of favorite leaders like Eli and Samuel, and of the more prominent rulers

---

[10] The split between the northern and southern tribes of the confederacy of the Hebrews occurred after the death of Solomon c. 950 B.C. The Northern Kingdom came to an end in 722 B.C. when Samaria, the capital, was taken by Sargon the King of Assyria. The Southern Kingdom survived about 140 years.

like Saul, David, Solomon and Ahab, which began
to be compiled during the two or three centuries
preceding the extinction of national independence.
It is possible also that about this same time little
collections of war songs and folk ditties began to
be made, likewise anonymous in their authorship,
which even after they had been committed to
writing continued chiefly to circulate orally.

In the eighth century before this era, however,
a movement sets in, beginning in the north and
spreading to the south, which was destined to
give the history of the Hebrew groups of tribes an
entirely new turn. Itinerant preachers arose who,
instead of flattering the rulers and pleasing the
people by comforting assurances of the protection of the national deity, denounce rulers and
people alike for political ambitions and for social
abuses. They set up as a new standard of fidelity
to Yahweh, obedience to moral precepts as against
mere ritual observances—sacrifices and expiatory
offerings—as a means of securing divine favor.
They announce the revolutionary doctrine that
Yahweh, in distinction from other gods, searches
the heart, is indifferent to sacrifice and invocation,
aye, rejects both unless those who approach Him
have clean hands and a clear conscience. These
preachers are known as *nebi'îm* "prophets," but
they give a new turn to the old designation, for
their prophecies are threats of impending national
disaster, instead of prognostications of the future
secured through an oracle or through some tradi-

tional method of divination, in connection with sacrifices as a bribe to make the deity well-disposed towards those who call upon him. Under the influence of these religious teachers, who continue to arise after the overthrow of the northern kingdom and who survive the fall of Jerusalem, the conception of the national deity Yahweh undergoes a profound change. Instead of the old conception of a willful and arbitrary deity, who favors his own people and who aids them in vanquishing their enemies, provided only rulers, priests and people combine in cajoling and flattering him, Yahweh is now viewed as a Power making for righteousness, who has set up certain standards of conduct and who rules by self-imposed laws of unbending justice. The upshot is the transformation of Yahwism into Judaism. Though at first the scope of this stern and just Deity was regarded as limited to his own people, it was a logical corollary that led in time to the conception of this new Yahweh as the single divine Power behind the manifestations of the universe, and controling the destinies of mankind in general.

## IV

### A NEW RELIGION AND ITS REFLEX IN LITERATURE

It is significant that this movement which ushers in a new religion arises at a time when the political decay of both kingdoms had begun to set in, through the perpetual menace of being swallowed up by one or the other of the two great powers of antiquity—Babylonia or Assyria on one side, and Egypt on the other. Judaism is not brought to fruition till the exhausted national life comes to a seemingly permanent close through the enforced exile of important elements of the Hebrew community to Babylonia after the capture of Jerusalem. Nebuchadnezzar, in thus following the policy inaugurated by Assyria, aimed to prevent a recrudescence of the national spirit. He succeeded, but his success was a factor in divorcing religion from nationality among the Hebrews, and led directly to the greatest contribution of the Hebrews to civilization—the creation of a spiritual form of religion with the conception of a just and righteous Creator of the universe as its central dogma, and with ethics as the test and as the main expression of the religious spirit. Judaism is the butterfly that bursts forth out of the chrysalis of Hebrew nationality.

A religious movement of large import is always accompanied by an intellectual stimulus, and we accordingly witness, as a result of such a stimulus given by the religious teachings of the prophets, a period of literary activity setting in during the sojourn of the best elements of the Hebrew people in Babylonia. The Yahwist and Elohist (and probably other) documents are combined with the codes that had been compiled and with the annals and records of the period of the loose confederacy—known as the days of the Judges—

and of the more closely knit union in the days of the two kingdoms, to form a continuous history from the creation of the world to the destruction of the southern kingdom.[11] What is more significant, the early myths and traditions as well as the genuine history are interpreted in the spirit of the prophets. Obedience to the ethical standards set up by the prophets in the name of Yahweh, now fast changing into the universal Jehovah, becomes the touchstone according to which the traditions and events of the past are judged. Those who stand the test, like the patriarchs, albeit purely fanciful creations of popular tradition, are held up as the models for all times. Disobedience is followed by punishment, and all the misfortunes of rulers and of the people, including visitations of disease and famine, defeats in battle and the final extinction of the national life, are regarded as the inevitable result of running counter to the high ethical standards set up by the prophets. In this endeavor, history is often distorted, and contradictions also result. Able rulers like Ahab are held up to scorn, because not answering to the ethical test. By the side of the historical and real David, a purely fictitious pious king arises to whom as a "sweet singer of Israel" religious compositions are ascribed, breathing a religious spirit that is quite foreign to the real David, and embodying sentiments far in advance of the age in which

---

[11] Forming the first division of the Old Testament, from Genesis to Kings.

47

he lived. The David to whom the Psalms are ascribed by an uncritical age is a figure irreconcilable with the David who is to be judged by the acts of his life and by his political policy. The traditions of the age of Solomon, marking a signal advance in the political and social growth of the united nation, undergo complete transformation with a view of making this most notable figure of the past conform to the teachings of the prophets. Solomon becomes a paragon of wisdom and, what is more, a pious devotee of Yahweh, impelled by his fine religious spirit to build a glorious temple in the capital city. He dedicates the edifice with a prayer that breathes the very essence of a highly spiritualized ethical faith in a God of universal scope. The real Solomon crops out in stories[12] which the compilers of historical documents were either unwilling to suppress, or which they retained because they did not recognize the contradiction which such tales presented to the wise and good king to whom were ascribed books in the O. T. collection, reflecting wisdom and a philosophical attitude towards life, like Proverbs and Koheleth.

## V

## THE FIRST GENUINE "AUTHORS"

A further and direct result of this literary activity was to bring the conception of authorship more into the foreground. The first genuine au-

---

[12] As *e.g.* of his harem and of his worshipping foreign deities (I Kings xi.) and of his heavy imposts on his people (chapter xii).

thors among the Hebrews were the prophets; not as yet in the Greek sense of claiming proprietorship in the written word, but in stamping their personality indelibly on the spoken one. For these religious guides and exhorters in the pre-exilic period were still speaking and not yet writing prophets. It is doubtful whether any of the group represented in the O. T. collection by the books of Amos, Hosea, Isaiah and Micah, *wrote* a single word of the prophecies ascribed to them. They spoke to the rulers and to the people as the opportunity presented itself. It may be that some of their utterances were taken down at the time, or shortly thereafter, by interested scribes, but for the greater part the preservation of such remains as we have of the warnings and instructions and denunciations of the pre-exilic prophets must have been due to the profound impression that they made on those who heard them. At a time when oral tradition was the chief means of preserving the recollection of events and utterances (as well as judicial decisions and the regulations of the cult), the human memory was strong and reliable; and this applies more particularly to what we may call the *collective* memory which forms the basis of oral tradition. At all events, the striking personality of the prophet, as the source of the impression made by him, leads him to be closely associated with *what* he says. The two—the prophet and his utterance—become bound up in each other. In the case of a judicial decision or an oracle, the judge and the diviner are merely mediums. They derive their authority from their supposed direct relationship to the deity as whose representatives they act. The collectors of traditions and the annalists do not project their personality into what they write down, but the prophet, though speaking in the name of Yahweh and because he is impelled by a hidden force to speak out even at the risk of danger to himself, yet gives to what he says a personal aspect which is, as already suggested, the keynote to his influence.

The speaking prophet, thus, in a very pertinent sense represents the beginning of authorship among the Hebrews—by virtue of this identification of his utterances with his personality.

Jeremiah, surviving the destruction of Jerusalem, marks the transition to the writing prophet, for the tradition which represents him as dictating his utterances to a scribe, though subsequent to their delivery, appears to be entirely reliable.[13] He writes letters[14] to the captives in Babylonia. When we come to Ezekiel, the great prophet of the captivity, the transformation from the speaking to the writing prophet is complete. Indeed, it is doubtful whether Ezekiel spoke at all. His chief activity consisted in writing his exhortations and instructions, and in circulating them through written copies;[15] while the orations of the later

---

[13] Jeremiah, xxxvi.    [14] Chapter xxix.
[15] Note particularly the last nine chapters of the Book of Ezekiel chapters xl–xlviii), detailing the plan for the rebuilding of the temple and of the reorganization of the cult, which clearly were intended to be read.

prophets, carrying us down into the third century, B.C., have all the earmarks of artistic literary compositions, written to be *read* rather than to be *heard*. The author, concerned for the form as much as for the matter, steps on the boards—and he has come to stay.

More than this, in the course of the further development of the written literature, the author becomes as important as what he writes, with the result of associating with the author the *authority* for the written document. When that stage has been reached, the tendency arises to ascribe the literary remains of the past to certain authors. Anonymity became unsatisfactory; it seemed to lack authority. Unless it was known who said something, how could one be sure of its value or its authenticity? Such was the profound change, superinduced through the emphasis laid upon authorship in the case of any composition, that anonymity which was formerly a source of strength now became a symptom of weakness. A book without an author appeared to be a body without a head, or rather a lifeless form which needed the spirit of the author to be breathed into it in order to awaken it to real life. The written word lost, as it were, its *raison d'être*, unless one knew who was behind the document. *Cherchez l'auteur* became an obligation resting upon those who wished to secure for the anonymous productions of the past the authority needed to preserve them as precious legacies. And so the search for authors began.

Authors had to be invented, in order to secure a sanction for what was to be found in documents that had been handed down from past ages. The name of the author became the trademark without which a literary product would not be recognized as genuine.

## VI

### TRADITIONAL "AUTHORSHIP"

It is a direct consequence of this change in the attitude towards the written word that led to the tradition which ascribed the Pentateuch in its completed form, as also the Book of Job, to Moses; Joshua and Samuel to the two leaders whose names their books bore; Kings and the Book of Lamentations to Jeremiah. In further development of this process, which was a gradual one stretching over a considerable period, Psalms were ascribed to David, and Proverbs, Koheleth and the Song of Songs to Solomon. The uncritical and unhistorical character of such a gradually evolving tradition need hardly be emphasized. In most cases we can follow the association of ideas which thus led to distributing the books of the sacred collection among a group of prominent figures of the past. Because the Pentateuch which became technically known as the "Five Books of the Law" was chiefly looked upon as a collection of laws, despite the fact that the greater part of it is taken up with narratives, it was attributed to Moses, he having become in tradition the law-giver *par excellence*. The tradition thus rested upon some semblance of historical justification, for there is no reason to question that Moses gave certain laws for the government of the nomadic tribes whom he molded into some kind of a political unit. These laws were in the forms of decisions. No doubt some of the provisions in the oldest code[16] represent in written form these early decisions, but it was, of course, an entirely uncritical procedure to ascribe *all* laws to Moses, and then to pass beyond this and make Moses the author of a series of books (containing among other things the description of his death), in which the codes were embodied.

The codes were originally separate from the narratives among which they are now interspersed, and themselves represent a gradual growth extending over many centuries. The longest and most important of these codes[17] cannot be earlier than 440 B.C.—about eight hundred years after Moses! To Moses was also ascribed the authorship of the Book of Job, merely because the prose story of Job (chapter i, ii), preceding the series of speeches by Job and his three visitors, appears to describe conditions that seemed to fit in with the patriarchal days which Moses is supposed to have described in the narratives in Genesis. Even more baseless is the view which made Joshua the author of the Book of Joshua and ascribed to Samuel

[16] This is the so-called Book of the Covenant (Exod. xx–xxiii, 19), dating from about the ninth century.

[17] The so-called Priestly Code, covering Leviticus and a large part of Numbers. The Deuteronomic Code (chapters xii–xxvi), now encased in a series of introductory and concluding addresses ascribed to Moses, with some historical or rather traditional data, dates from the seventh century.

the books of Samuel, merely because in the books
in question Joshua and Samuel appear as the
prominent figures. To David the Psalms are
ascribed because the tradition about David made
him a poet as well as a soldier. Poetic gifts and
warlike qualities are not unusual companions.
The warrior in the ancient East, free from conventional restraint, is apt to be a romantic character.
The narratives of David emphasize this trait, and
there is nothing improbable in the supposition
that he also composed poems, but these poems, we
may be sure, recited his own exploits and those of
his ancestors. They were martial in character, not
religious. The lament over Jonathan, embodied
in the narrative of Saul and David[18] *may* have been
written by David, at least in part, but to picture
David as a composer of hymns, embodying the
highest religious sentiments, and expressing the
longings and aspirations of a finely attuned religious soul, wrapped up in a semi-mystic attachment
to a God conceived in the spirit of the prophets,
shows the length to which an uncritical tradition
could go in the endeavor to relieve compositions
of anonymity.

In the case of Proverbs there is at least a logical link between the worldly wisdom underlying
many of the sayings of the collection, and the reputation for wisdom and sound judgment which
Solomon acquired. There is no reason to question
the authenticity of this view of Solomon, even

---

[18] II Samuel i. 19–27.

though the stories told in the Book of Kings[19] in illustration of the king's fine sense of justice and his skill in reaching a decision may be the fanciful inventions of a later age. But many of the Proverbs again convey religious and ethical ideals far in advance of the age of Solomon, and show that the tradition ascribing the collection to him is primarily due again to the desire to hit upon some individual who seemed appropriate as the probable or possible author. For the Song of Songs—a collection of love ditties of purely secular origin, which, through an artificial exegesis, under the form of an allegorical interpretation were invested with a religious purport[20]—it seemed sufficient ground for a naïve tradition to name Solomon as the author, because the Bridegroom is likened to a king[21]—and Solomon was the king *par excellence*. Similarly, because Koheleth, the writer of Ecclesiastes, calls himself "a king in Jerusalem," tradition fixed upon Solomon as the author. The author indeed *meant* to represent himself as Solomon, and with this in view chose a thin disguise in order not to fall under the charge of deliberately practicing a deception on his readers. Jeremiah, the

---

[19] *e.g.* I Kings iii. 16–28—the judgment of Solomon in the dispute over the child claimed by two women.

[20] The lover was pictured as Yahweh and the beloved as Israel, or, in the Christian exegesis, the Bridegroom became Christ, and the Bride the church.

[21] The real significance of the comparison lies in the custom still found among the village inhabitants of Palestine to hail the groom and bride as king and queen. The wedding festivities, lasting for a week, take on the form of an homage, by means of processions, dances and jollification, in honor of the couple, masquerading as king and queen.

prophet of gloom, who bewails the destruction of his people, even while announcing the downfall of the Southern Kingdom as inevitable, is naturally selected as the author of the book of Lamentations, as he seemed to be also an appropriate figure to whom to attach the compilation of the Book of Kings.

## VII

### THE GROWTH OF THE SACRED COLLECTION

It has already been suggested that this process of assigning authors to the books comprising a sacred collection was one of gradual growth, as the formation of the collection itself was the result of a long process that did not reach its termination till the end of the first century of our era. We cannot say exactly when the process began. We know that Ezra brought a code back with him from Babylonia about 440 B.C. and read it to the assembled people at Jerusalem. It was represented as being the law which Moses had given his people at Yahweh's command, but there is no indication as yet that the entire Pentateuch was already in existence in its present form, or if it were that it was ascribed to Moses as the single author. The tradition attributing the Pentateuch as a whole to Moses, therefore, does not date further back in any case than the fourth century B.C. and probably did not take definite shape till a century or so later. Moses is not named as the author in the Pentateuch itself, any more than an author is named in the Books of Joshua, Judges, Samuel or

Kings. The headings or titles in the case of Psalms are all later than the compositions themselves. Many of them have no headlines at all,[22] while quite a number mention other names than David as the author[23]—a proof that the tradition ascribing them all to David was not yet definite in the first century before this era, which is the earliest date which we can fix for the final reduction of the five books of Psalms in their present form. This conclusion as to the lateness of the rise of tradition ascribing authors to Biblical books is confirmed by Proverbs—compiled not earlier than the middle of the third century B.C.—since some of the chapters, according to the headings, are distinctly ascribed to others than to Solomon.[24] For Koheleth and the Song of Songs we have merely the late titles as the indication of authorship. Since the composition of these two books, likewise, belongs to a late period, all the evidence obliges us to pass close to the beginning of our era for the completion of the process which established a definite authorship for *all* the books of the sacred collection.

Bearing in mind that, as has been pointed out, genuine authorship arises among the Hebrews with the great prophets of the eighth and succeeding centuries, and becomes definite with the transi-

---

[22] So, *e.g.*, Psalms i, ii, x, xxxiii, xliii, lxxi, xciii–xcvii, civ–cvii, etc.

[23] So, *e.g.*, Psalms xlii, xliv, xlvi–xlix, lxxxiv–lxxxv, are ascribed to the sons of Korah; l and lxxiii–lxxxiii to Asaph; lxxii to Solomon; xc to Moses, etc. Others mention no author in the headline, *e.g.*, Psalms lxvi–lxvii.

[24] Chapter xxv to the "Men of Hezekiah"; Chapter xxx to Agur; Chapter xxi to Lemuel.

tion from the speaking to the writing prophet, we should expect a more reliable tradition to have arisen in connection with that portion of the Old Testament which embodies the utterance of the prophets of pre-exilic, exilic and post-exilic times. That in considerable measure is actually the case, but it is interesting to note that precisely in this part of the collection we come across the first instances of pseudepigraphy, that is to say, literary compositions in the style of a prophet and issued under the authority of his name. The Book of Isaiah furnishes the most conspicuous example. It represents a collection of carefully worked out orations covering a period of at least three hundred years, all placed under the name of Isaiah, who flourished during the last quarter of the eighth century B.C. The genuine Isaiah stands out preeminent for his eloquence and his power. It was, therefore, a name to conjure with; and hence under Isaiah were grouped, in addition to the genuine utterances of the pre-exilic teacher—constituting hardly more than a fifth of the present compass of the book[25]—compositions of high literary merit but which bear the earmarks of the exilic and post-exilic period to which they belong. They were clearly written for the consolation and en-

---

[25] The genuine Isaiahanic portions are to be found in the first half of the book; they are chiefly chapters i–xii (though with later insertions); xx and portions of xvii, xviii, xxii and xxviii–xxxii. Chapters xl–lxvi are entirely exilic and post-exilic, consisting of several collections that once existed independently and were then combined and added to the first part of Isaiah. See for a brief summary of the present state of the problem, Gray, "Critical Introduction to the Old Testament," pp. 178–188.

couragement of the pious community and aimed
to give expression to the religious ideals of the
prophets and to regulate the life of the community
according to these standards. They were not the
fiery denunciations of the prophet directly address-
ing his hearers, impelled to speak out the thoughts
that burned within him and to voice the desires
and hopes which consumed his being. Even when
these later compositions struck the note of despair
and of uncompromising criticism of the policy of
political or religious leaders, the mark of the
written composition was unmistakable. What was
thus composed in the spirit of Isaiah, what echoed
his hopes and reflected his ideals, even what consciously imitated his style was looked upon as
worthy of finding a place with the genuine utterances. It is not only indicative of the absence of
the historical sense which thus led compilers to
ascribe to Isaiah productions that arose generations and centuries after he had passed away, but
also of the still inchoate conception of authorship. The author had made his appearance, but
his position remained for a time somewhat uncertain. The impression of the personality had begun
to predominate, but as a survival of the earlier age
when *what* was said was considered more important
than *who* said it, what *might* have been said by
some striking personality was without much hesitation placed in the class with what a more or less
reliable tradition regarded as having actually been
said by him.

There is not a single book in that portion of the Old Testament devoted to the collections of the utterances and orations of the prophets which does not contain considerable additions. Even in such short books as that of Jonah, consisting of four chapters, and of Obadiah, consisting of only one "vision"—the technical term for a prophetic utterance—there are insertions, while in longer books like Amos, Hosea and Micah for the pre-exilic period and Nahum, Joel, Zephaniah and Zechariah for the post-exilic age, the additions are considerable. The last of the prophets in the present order, strangely enough, writes under a *nom de plume*, Malachi.[26] All these books are still essentially *compilations,* in which it was considered entirely proper to include utterances, irrespective of their origin, which seemed to be appropriate. The book of Ezekiel shows more unity than any other of the prophetical books, though this book also includes portions that do not belong to Ezekiel, while in the case of the Book of Jeremiah —a combination of orations with a historical narrative—the extraneous parts are again considerable. We can thus trace in the editing process itself which gradually through the labors of various editors produced the prophetical books, the further evolution of literary production through the stage of pseudepigraphy after the conception of the author had arisen.

[26] Malachi means "My Messenger." The name is taken from Chapter iii. 1, "Behold, I send my messenger." The three chapters bearing this name date from about the middle of the fifth century B.C.

In a certain sense the final stage of this process marked by a scrupulous regard for handing down in authentic form the exact words of an author was never reached. The historical sense was lacking even in the first century of our era when the canon of the Old Testament was finally fixed by learned but entirely uncritical Rabbis, who looked upon tradition as the final court of appeal. The rise of this tradition, which we have seen, led to ascribing the authorship of many of the books of the sacred collections to certain figures of the past through incidental association of ideas with these men; or, on even more baseless grounds, is in itself a proof that these Rabbis were as yet not far removed from the age which considered itself justified in editing the literary remains of ancient prophets by inserting verses, sections, chapters and entire groups of chapters that belonged to a period other than the one in which the prophet flourished. Without a critical and historical sense, such as the Greeks alone among the peoples of antiquity possessed in so striking a degree, a complete sense of the significance of authorship could not arise. If we accept the other alternative, and assume that those who fixed the canon had such a sense, we should be forced to accuse them of willful deception, aye, of literary forgery when, for example, they claimed for Moses the authorship of the Pentateuch, and for David the authorship of the Psalms; or for Solomon the authorship of Proverbs, Song of Songs and Koheleth; and so on through the list.

They are saved from this serious charge by their naïveté in accepting unreliable traditions. We may feel quite sure that if Johanan ben Zakkai, the most distinguished of the group that settled at Jamnia (or Jabneh), where the canon was fixed at the end of the first century A.D., could be brought out of his grave and the question put to him whether he really meant that Moses wrote the Pentateuch, (including the description of his own death)[27] and that Solomon wrote the Proverbs, that everything in the book of Isaiah was written by Isaiah, he would be amazed at a query that would appear unintelligible to him, because involving a conception of authorship that had not yet been reached in the uncritical age to which he belonged, and which also lacked the true historical sense.

## VIII

### KOHELETH AS A *NOM DE PLUME*

Having thus sketched the growth of literary production among the Hebrews from anonymity to the rise of the conception of authorship, and through this to the stage of naïve pseudepigraphy and to the formation of an uncritical and unhistorical tradition regarding the authors of the books of a sacred collection, we are prepared to assign the Book of Koheleth to its proper place, and we are also ready to make the attempt of separating the original portions of the book from the additions and

---

[27] To explain this strange detail, the Rabbis assumed that Joshua added the last eight verses of Deuteronomy.

modifications to which, in common with all of the books of the sacred collection, it was exposed.

The first thing that strikes us in the book is that the author speaks of himself. "I, Koheleth, was king over Israel in Jerusalem" (i. 12). This notice does not occur at the beginning, but in the body of the book. It is all the more reliable because it is *not* a heading, for the headings to all the books of the O. T. are later additions, as are the titles of the Psalms and the headlines to the chapters in the collections of the prophets. These headings and titles are, therefore, of no value in determining the period to which a book belongs or of the circumstances under which it was written. A reference, however, to an author within a book is a valuable index; and its value is increased when we find such a reference to be unique. That is in fact the case. Most of the books of the O. T.—as the Pentateuch and all the historical books, as well as Job, Esther, Daniel and Ruth—have not even headings.[28] The book of Koheleth is the *only one* in which an author speaks of himself by name or in the first person. The closest analogy is in the case of the prophets who use the first person when describing a vision,[29] or in connection with the divine message which they receive,[30] but they never speak of themselves by name. The introduction of the name is an indication that we have passed the period of

---

[28] The headings are found only in the case of Psalms, Proverbs, Song of Songs, Koheleth and Nehemiah and in the collections of the prophets.
[29] *e.g.*, Isaiah vi.
[30] So constantly, Ezekiel.

anonymity and have reached the point when it became customary, though not as yet essential, to associate a literary production with some individual. The book is no longer common property, and this leads us to the period subsequent to the appearance of the great prophets in the eighth century with whom, as we have seen,[31] authorship in any real sense begins among the Hebrews.

We may further conclude that Koheleth belongs to a transition period. The process leading from anonymity in literary production to a definite sense of authorship is not yet complete. This follows from the fact that Koheleth is not a genuine name but a disguise for the real author. It is not until about 180 B.C. that we come across a book *with* an author among the Jews, as we should call the people after the exilic period in contradistinction to "Hebrews," which is the proper designation in the pre-exilic age. About that year a certain Jesus Ben Sira issued under his name a collection of sayings which was translated into Greek by his grandson about fifty years later and became known as Ecclesiasticus, though the more proper designation is "The Wisdom of Ben Sira."[32] This book was not included in the sacred canon but found a place in the supplementary collection known as the "Apocrypha." That the work of Ben

---

[31] Above, p. 49 *et seq.*

[32] Until quite recently the Hebrew original was lost. Large portions of it were discovered by the late Solomon Schechter and were embodied in a special work, "Fragments of the Hebrew Original of the Wisdom of Ben Sira," by S. Schechter and C. Taylor (Cambridge, 1899).

Sira was not regarded as worthy of a place in the
sacred collection was due in part to its late date
(though the Book of Daniel and many of the Psalms
are of still later origin) but in larger part to the
very fact that it appeared with the name of its
author attached. Had Ben Sira issued it anonymously or had he conveyed the impression that it
was the work of Solomon, it would have stood a
good chance of forming a second book of Proverbs,
for the spirit is much the same as in these books, and
some of the sayings are just as fine and as striking
as the earlier collection to which tradition had
attached the name of the famous and wise king.

Koheleth lived at a time when the author
had begun to be a factor in the intellectual and
social life, but still could hide himself under a
*nom de plume* and reap an advantage from so
doing. For Koheleth *is* a disguise and it is reasonable to suppose that in describing himself as a
king over Jerusalem, who had amassed wealth,
who possessed great power and who was also
"wiser than all who were before me in Jerusalem"
(i. 16), he aimed to identify himself with Solomon
whose name must, therefore, have already become
at the time when Koheleth wrote a synonym for
wisdom, glory and power. The device was successful. An uncritical tradition, accepting the implication in the disguise, attributed the book to
Solomon. The magic of this name went a large way
towards overcoming the objections that later arose
against its inclusion in the canon because of its

heterodox spirit and contents. The name Koheleth thus furnishes an instance of real pseudepigraphy among the Jews. We may acquit the author of any desire to deceive his readers, and he certainly did not look forward to having his book included in a sacred collection, but apart from the hope which may have tickled his vanity of increasing both the popularity and the influence of his book by creating the impression that he was speaking in the name of the wise and glorious king, he may have been actuated in adopting a *nom de plume* by the fear of risking a personal unpopularity through his identification with the teachings which he set forth in such bold fashion. The author may not have been of the stuff of which martyrs are made. Authors rarely are. He would, at all events, have been condemned by the pious and the orthodox, and his book after creating a mild sensation would probably have been consigned to oblivion. Instead of being included in a sacred collection, it might have been placed on an *Index Librorum prohibitorum* and the world would have been the poorer for the loss. We should, therefore, be grateful for the device which he adopted as well as for its complete success, indicated by the heading at the beginning of the book, which was subsequently added, and in which the words "son of David" were included so as to remove all doubt of the identification of Koheleth with the famous king.

But how can we be so certain of the name Koheleth having been chosen as a disguise? In the first place, we know that there was no Hebrew king of that name, just as there was no "King Lemuel" who appears as the author of the last chapter of Proverbs, and whose name is likewise a disguise; and secondly, Koheleth does not represent a formation in Hebrew, which could be used as the name of an individual. The word is composed of four consonants, KHLT,[33] the last of which is the indication of a feminine noun.

This of itself forbids us to regard the word as the name of a man. Hebrew proper names, as proper names in other Semitic languages, are composed of a verb with the name of a deity as the subject— expressed or implied—to which a noun may be attached as an object. Thus Nathaniel, meaning "God has given," originally had a noun like "son" attached to it; and such a name was further abbreviated to Nathan, by the omission of the name of the deity. David, meaning "Beloved" was originally "Beloved of Yah."[34] Jerubbaal, meaning "Baal has added" was originally "Baal has added a son." Joseph, meaning "he adds," is abbreviated from the fuller name, which may have been "God adds a son." Now a form like Koheleth from an underlying stem KHL meaning "to gather," and with an ending T attached, would have abstract or collective force as "gathering" or "assembly." This was the meaning taken by

---

[33] Only the consonants are written in the Hebrew script. The vowel signs were subsequently added, and in Hebrew manuscripts do not appear.
[34] A form of the name "Yahweh."

the one who translated the book into Greek,[35] and with the book also the name of the author—Ecclesiastes, which can hardly be rendered otherwise than "an assembly man" or as we might put it "assembly [or church] speaker." The Greek translator appears to have followed Jewish tradition, which likewise explained the term as "preacher." The term however might also (be) be rendered as "assembler" or "collector." Less plausible are other suggestions proposed for the name as "academy," "narrator," "member of an assembly" and the like.[36] Whichever of these explanations we adopt, it is evident that Koheleth is not the genuine name of an individual, but an artificial designation.

Ernest Renan suggested[37] that each of the four letters represented the beginning of a word, so that the name would be the abbreviation of a sentence, but since it is impossible to determine what the words were, the conjecture does not carry us very far. If, as seems certain, the author intended to have us believe that Koheleth was Solomon, then in some way the four letters K H L T ought to be a disguise for Sh L M H which are the four consonants of the name Solomon in its Hebrew form. The common manner in which words are disguised in Hebrew is to substitute, for the correct

---

[35] Hardly earlier than the close of the first century of our era.

[36] See the discussion of the name in Renan's "L'Ecclésiaste" (Paris, 1890), pp. 11 *et seq.* and Barton's "Commentary to the Book of Ecclesiastes," pp. 67–68.

[37] In the Introduction to his French translation of Koheleth, "L'Ecclésiaste" (Paris, 1890), p. 6.

consonants, others chosen according to some system as, for example, to take in place of the first
consonant in the alphabetical order the last, in
place of the second the one before the last, and so
on. But neither this system nor any other cipher
leads to any satisfactory result. A name may,
however, also be disguised by starting from the
meaning of the underlying stem, and replacing
that stem by another that is synonymous. The
stem Sh LM which underlies Solomon signifies
"to be complete," "to be whole," and this comes
close to "gather" and "assemble" which we have
seen is the meaning of the stem K H L. Both
Sh LMH and KHLT, moreover, have the feminine
ending which in Hebrew is either H or T. It may
be, therefore, that this association of ideas led the
author to the disguise chosen by him.

More important, however, than the explanation of the name, pleasant though it would be to
find an entirely satisfactory one, is the fact that
the author chose a *nom de plume*. This suggests
that the age in which he wrote stands midway
between the beginning of authorship among the
Hebrews and the completion of the process, represented by Jesus Ben Sira who, as we have seen,
is the first actually to issue a book under his name.
Koheleth belongs, therefore, to a time when names
were associated with literary productions, but
before the period when this had become the conventional practice on the part of authors. This nar-
rows the range of the possible date of composition

of the book to the three centuries between the end of the exilic period and the time of Jesus Ben Sira. That the age of Ben Sira (*c.*180 B.C.) is the *terminus ad quem* for the composition of Ecclesiastes is now definitely established through the discovery of large parts of the Hebrew original of his "sayings," which reveal his dependence upon Koheleth both in thought and in language.[38] The relationship is at times so close as to amount virtually to a quotation from Koheleth on the part of Ben Sira, and the evidence is complete that Ben Sira utilizes Koheleth and not *vice versa*.

We are led to the post-exilic period, *i.e.*, after 500 B.C., for the composition of the book by the further consideration of the successful device of the author in having his book ascribed to Solomon, for the Solomon of tradition, who becomes an author, rests upon the growth of legend around that illustrious figure, which transformed him from a very worldly figure to a type of wisdom and piety. This transformation belongs to the post-exilic age. To be sure, even in the post-exilic Book of Kings in which the monarch is idealized, his fondness for women and his introduction of foreign cults are not entirely suppressed, but they are glossed over as due to the weaknesses of his old age.[39] The apologetic aim is evident, as is the further contradiction between the real and the traditional Solomon

---

[38] The reader will find the proof succinctly set forth in Barton's "Commentary" pp. 53–56, and also in McNeile's "Introduction to Ecclesiastes" pp. 34–39.

[39] I Kings xi.

in the scene between his successor Rehoboam and the representatives of the people who ask to be relieved of the taxations and hard service which Solomon had put upon them[40]. This picture ill accords with the policy of a virtuous and god-fearing ruler. It is evident that it is not the historical figure but the idealized, unhistorical Solomon of the post-exilic period who comes to be regarded as the author to whom Proverbs, Song of Songs and Koheleth are attributed. The necessity for making Solomon, as the supposed author of these books, accord with the figure of tradition, led in the case of the Song of Songs to an allegorical interpretation so as to disguise the secular and indeed sensual character of these charming love ditties. In the case of Koheleth, it led to large additions in order to tone down the main two features of the book, namely, the reflection that life is vanity, and the advice to enjoy the material pleasures of life as the best way of spending one's days.

## IX

### THE ADDITIONS TO KOHELETH

The character of these additions is unmistakable. Let us take up a few illustrations. Koheleth, in accord with the idealized figure of Solomon, represents himself as having acquired "wisdom and knowledge" greater than any of his predecessors.[41] He then resolves to make a test of

---

[40] Chapter xii.
[41] Chapter i. 16. The picture is clearly based on I Kings v. 9–11.

frivolity and foolishness"[42] as the direct opposite
of wisdom and knowledge, only to find out that
this was futile, "chasing after wind" as the picturesque phrase runs. Now, it would not be consistent with the dignity of a wise king to represent him
as deliberately following foolish pursuits. So, in
order to save his reputation, the word "wisdom" is
inserted to suggest that by virtue of his pursuing
also wisdom, he ascertained the emptiness of
"frivolity and foolishness." Similarly, when Koheleth in the course of his career also decides to make
a test of riotous living (ii. 3), the commentator
adds "my mind acting with wisdom," to indicate
that the wise and pious Solomon did not throw
himself madly into sensual delights, but solely as
a test.

Still more striking are the additions consistently introduced after the conclusion is reached to
"eat, drink, and be merry." Koheleth argues[43]
why spend one's life in hard work when at the end
of it all one must leave one's wealth to someone
who has not labored for it? Is not life vain if spent
in days of toil and nights of worry? Therefore—
enjoy thyself, and look upon this as the aim of life,
approved by God. This is strange advice, indeed,
to be offered by the wise and pious Solomon; and,
accordingly, a commentator adds that the capacity
for the enjoyment of life is "a gift of God" be-
stowed only on the virtuous, whereas the sinner is

[42] Chapter i. 17.
[43] Chapter ii. 20–25.

punished by being obliged to toil and to leave enjoyment to the virtuous (ii. 26). The contradiction to the trend of Koheleth's thought is as manifest as is the sophistry in the implication that only the good can enjoy life, and that the virtuous are not apt to fall heir to tainted money.

When again Koheleth contends that, since things cannot be changed in this world from the manner in which God made them, one should enjoy what there is (iii. 12-14), the commentator adds that "God has so made [the world] that man will fear Him" (iii. 14$^b$)—thus rather skillfully giving a reverent turn to Koheleth's cynical reflection. Again, when towards the end of the book Koheleth once more reaches the conclusion that life without enjoyment is vain, that one should follow one's inclinations and satisfy all one's desires, the antidote to such teachings is given in the added warning, "But know that for all these things God will bring thee into judgment" (xi. 9)— a reflection which is as far removed from Koheleth's point of view as heaven is from earth.

Our commentator pursues his double purpose to the bitter end; (1) to make the picture of Solomon accord with the traditional figure of the wise and God-fearing king and (2) to lend the weight of Solomon's name to counteract the objectionable and dangerous conclusions reached by Koheleth. Accordingly, when Koheleth closes his book by the assertion "all is vanity" (xii. 8) the pious commentator adds "Fear God and observe his

commandments, for this [applies to] every man"
(xii. 13).

These illustrations will suffice to enable us
to detect such additions whenever they occur.
They meet us at every turn.[44] For the most part
they are brief as when, in the midst of an argument
that the purpose of God in making the world is
past finding out, the commentator to counteract
such irreverent pessimism insists "God has made
everything beautiful in its season" (iii. 11[a]), or
when Koheleth in a cynical spirit urges us to put no
confidence in dreams, the opportunity is seized upon
to give the advice, "Fear God" (v. 6). To counteract the gloomy reflection that "the day of death
is better than the day of birth," the saying is
inserted "better is a [good] name than fine oil"
(vii. 1). When Koheleth, consistent with his point
of view, advises against being either too bad or too
good, for either will bring one into trouble, the
commentator in his optimistic spirit adds that "he
who fears God will steer clear of everything" *i.e.*,
will avoid all difficulties (vii. 18[b]). Not infrequently, however, the additions are more elaborate.
To furnish the answer to Koheleth's contention,
based upon his experience, that in this topsy-turvy
world the wicked are buried amidst pomp, whereas
the righteous are forgotten, the pious commentator
enters upon an elaborate argument (viii. 11-13), to
show that even if justice is not always promptly

---

[44] In the brief comments to the translation I have indicated them,
and, in order to give a general view of their character, I have put them
together in the Appendix.

meted out, "it shall not be well for the wicked" and that virtue will find its reward—which is percisely the *contrary* of what Koheleth asserts, not only in this place but elsewhere.

Of special interest are additions in which the style of Koheleth is deliberately imitated, so as to make the conformity to the traditional Solomon more plausible. Koheleth has just declared[45] that justice is often perverted in this world and that the wicked are enthroned in the seat of the righteous. Such a sentiment is entirely out of place in the mouth of a king famed for his righteous judgment, and so the traditional Solomon is made to add, "But I reflected that God will judge both the righteous and the wicked, for there is an appointed time for every occurrence and for every act" (iii. 17). This sentiment, the close of which is reminiscent of iii. 1, is put precisely in the manner of Koheleth and with conscious intent, as is also the addition at the close of the seventh chapter, where after Koheleth has given voice to a particularly striking bit of cynicism that whereas one might discover a genuine man in a crowd of a thousand, one will not find a decent woman, the pious commentator tries to tone down the thought by making Koheleth say, "Besides, however, I have found this, that God has made man straight, but they have devised many contrivances" (vii. 29) by which the original fine nature of man is perverted. In this way God is at least relieved from the initial responsibility for

---

[45] Chapter iii. 16.

75

the worthlessness of most men and of all women. The addition is in keeping with the conventional view of man's fall from grace by sin, as illustrated in the third chapter of Genesis.

## X

### THE PROVERBS APPENDED TO KOHELETH

But besides these additions—made in the interest of maintaining intact the figure of Solomon as the type of the virtuous and God-fearing king, after he had become associated with the book of Koheleth as its author, and to offer the antidote to the poisonous teachings of the real Koheleth— there are also scattered throughout the book sayings and maxims, generally in praise of the advantages of wisdom and of the qualities of the wise man, which are introduced again with a double aim, to strengthen the plausibility of Solomon, the supposed compiler of the Book of Proverbs, being also the author of Koheleth, and to further counteract some of the heretical teachings and, more particularly, the skeptical and cynical spirit pervading the entire book. These additions, of which there are considerably more[46] than of the class just discussed, are entirely in the style of the Book of Proverbs and might indeed have been included in that collection. Where do they come from? Evidently the collection of sayings in our

---

[46] They cover about 40 verses or about one-sixth of the entire book which consists of 222 verses, as against about 25 verses covered by the additions of the pious commentator. They are indicated in every instance in the comments to the translation, and are also put together in the appendix.

Book of Proverbs did not exhaust the extant literature of this character. The collection represents
rather a selection of what were considered the
best sayings, worthy of being ascribed to a king
typifying wisdom. From the statement in the
Book of Kings that Solomon "spoke three thousand
proverbs, and his songs were a thousand and five,"[47]
which already assumes the existence of the tradition that ascribed Proverbs and the Song of
Songs to the king, we may be permitted to conclude that there were other literary productions
extant in the post-exilic period of a gnomic and
lyrical character. Because *some* such compositions
came to be ascribed to Solomon, it was concluded
with the naïveté characteristic of an entirely uncritical age that *all* such literature was the work of
Solomon. Not satisfied with this, some glossater
to the Book of Kings went his predecessors one
better and asserted *ad majorem gloriam regis* that
the extant animal and tree fables were also of
Solomonic origin.[48] The passage in the Book of
Kings is manifestly later than the period when a
collection of Proverbs existed which was ascribed
to Solomon. That collection was not necessarily the
one in our present Book of Proverbs, which would
bring us down into the third century, B.C., but was
at all events a portion of it. We must assume the

---

[47] I Kings v. 12.
[48] I Kings v. 13. "He spoke of trees from the cedar of Lebanon to the
hyssop springing from the wall; also of beasts, fowl, creeping things and fishes."
The passage is interesting as pointing at that time to the spread of such animal
and tree fables from their probable birthplace in distant India.

existence of such a collection ascribed to Solomon, prior to the insertion of sayings and maxims of the same general character in another book of which likewise Solomon was reputed to be the author.

These considerations lead us to the period after the compilation of the Book of Proverbs for the addition of such sayings to the Book of Kohe-leth. It does not necessarily follow that the original Book of Koheleth is also later than Proverbs, but the probabilities are strongly in favor of this conclusion, which is confirmed from other considerations. At all events, before these maxims and sayings were inserted, the tradition had been established that Koheleth *was* Solomon, as had also the belief that Solomon as the wise king was associated with the writing of proverbs to such an extent that all proverbial sayings were looked upon as Solo-monic, in the same sense that all laws came to be regarded as Mosaic. So close was the association between Solomon and the inditing of maxims, especially such as illustrated wisdom from various angles, that it not only seemed perfectly natural to add maxims to a book ascribed to the wise king, but such additions furnished to a later but still uncritical age a further proof of the Solomonic authorship of the book into which they were inserted. The "vicious circle" which is part and parcel of an uncritical age is thus made complete.

Now, how can we be sure that the maxims scattered through the book of Ecclesiastes actually represent later additions, made to strengthen the

authenticity of the Solomonic authorship and to
make the teachings of the book more palatable to
the orthodox believers in a good world created by
a power that rewards the virtuous and punishes
the evil-doer? What is the criterion for separating
the original components of the book of Koheleth
from the elements subsequently added? In the
case of the insertions intended to make the picture
of Solomon conform to the type of the virtuous and
god-fearing king and, incidentally, also to counteract the heretical views and implications of the
book, the general criterion is the manifest *inconsistency* of the utterances of Koheleth with the
pious reflections that were added whenever Koheleth gave voice to some particularly striking or
shocking sentiment. The same author could not
rail against prevailing wickedness and injustice,
and in the same breath declare that a just Providence presides over the universe. The pessimist
who sees black everywhere cannot be the same as
the one who finds everything good and beautiful.
The skeptic who asserts that all—the good and bad
alike—share a common fate (ix. 2) cannot be identical with the pious believer who is confident that
God will bring man to judgment for all his acts,
the hidden and the manifest (xi. 9 and xii. 14).

For the other class of insertions, enlarging
upon the aspects and qualities of wisdom, and in
other ways elaborating and modifying Koheleth's
reasonings and conclusions, the test is to be found
chiefly in the *interruption* of the context or of the

argument, and secondly, in the *form* of the maxims
and sayings, which marks them off sharply from
the original text. So, for instance, in the first chapter we have an example of a saying added after
the refrain that "all is vanity and chasing after
wind." After the fourteenth verse we read

> "The crooked cannot be straightened,
> And the lacking cannot be supplied."

The maxim has no direct connection with the
thought expressed by Koheleth, who is arguing
that it is foolish to investigate the mysteries of
the universe. The impulse to do so is a "sorry
business," for it merely leads one to see the vanity
of all things. To add that things cannot be changed
is a reflection to which Koheleth would probably
have assented, but it takes us away from his main
thought, to wit, that investigation by itself shows
that all things in this world are empty bubbles.
When a little further on (ii. 13), Koheleth reaches
the conclusion that wisdom seems to be better than
foolishness, at least to the extent that light is preferable to darkness, the insertion of a saying

> "The wise man has his eyes in his head,
> But the fool walks in darkness,"

giving expression to the somewhat trite thought
that a wise man sees what he is doing, whereas the
foolish one gropes about, furnishes an illustration
to the sentiment just expressed, but it interrupts
the context. The point which Koheleth urges is
that the advantage of wisdom over folly is only

an apparent superiority, for the fool and the wise man share the same fate. Both are forgotten and the one dies just as does the other.

Almost in direct contradiction to the thought of Koheleth is another insertion which we find in the fourth chapter, where he concludes that the endeavor of a man to outstrip his neighbor is likewise "vanity and a chasing after wind." The saying that follows (iv. 5)

"The fool folds his hands and consumes his own flesh"

is entirely out of the picture, whereas the next verse that "a handful of quiet is better than two handfuls in toil and chasing after wind," is fully in keeping with the context. The interruption of the thought is no less apparent in the saying (vi. 7)

"All the toil of a man is for his mouth,
And yet the appetite is never satisfied,"

which has no connection with what precedes or with what follows. Koheleth has been trying to show that a large family and a long life offer no compensation, unless one has enjoyed oneself during the span of one's existence. The reflection that one cannot get enough enjoyment is rather in the nature of an antidote to the doctrine of pleasure as the main thing in life, and shows that the commentator who added this saying was in sympathy with the point of view represented by the one (or by those) who added the pious comments in order to give an orthodox turn to Koheleth's teachings. Immediately after the inserted saying, the genuine

Koheleth once more appears with his question, "What is the advantage of being wise?" (vi. 8.)

In many cases, the insertions betray themselves as such by being manifestly suggested through a purely incidental reference to wisdom in contrast to foolishness. The commentator, who had perhaps a collection of proverbs before him, could not resist the temptation of selecting some sayings in further illustration, though not infrequently the supposed "illustration" carries us away from the thought that Koheleth had in mind. So, *e.g.*, Koheleth suggests in a pessimistic mood that the end of life is better than the beginning (vii. 8), and argues further that it is better to go to a funeral than to a banquet, for in a house of mourning you may hear some reasonable talk, whereas in a house of mirth you encounter fools (vii. 2 and 4). Our commentator, intent upon adding maxims in illustration or in supposed illustration of the text, steps in at this point (vii. 5-6)

> "It is better to hear the rebuke of a wise man,
> than to listen to the praise of fools.
> For as the crackling of thorns under a pot,
> so is the laughter of fools."

Koheleth has not been speaking of "rebuke" or "praise," nor is he concerned at this point with showing the foolishness of fools. He takes that for granted. Entirely out of the picture is the next insertion which follows (vii. 7)

> "Extortion deprives a wise man of reason
> and a bribe corrupts the mind,"

clearly superinduced because of the reference to the wise man who may be found in a house of mourning (vii. 4). Again, when Koheleth, continuing his train of thought (vii. 8), declares that the end of things is better than the beginning, there is no connection whatsoever with the two insertions (vii. 8$^b$-9)

> (*a*) "Better patience than haughtiness"
> (*b*) "Do not be prone to anger,
>       for anger endures [only] in the bosom of fools."

In the same chapter we find three further sayings in proof of the superiority of wisdom, which interrupt the context. They have not the slightest connection with either Koheleth's arguments or with his conclusions, and are suggested by purely incidental references to wisdom

> "Wisdom is better [49] than an inheritance,"
>    and an advantage to the living" (vii. 11).
> "For the protection of wisdom is (as strong) as the protection of silver,
>    And the advantage of knowledge [50] is that it gives life to those who possess it" (vii. 12).
> "Wisdom makes a wise man stronger than the ten rulers of a city" (vii. 19).

Again, at the beginning of the eighth chapter which advises caution in one's attitude towards a king who will always do what he likes, the "maxim" commentator takes advantage of the advice, which

---

[49] For this translation, see the comment to the passage.
[50] A variant adds "wisdom."

is offered in an ironical and somewhat cynical
spirit, to insert two sayings (viii. 1)

(*a*) "Who is like the wise man, and who knows
    [as he does] the explanation of a matter?"
(*b*) "The wisdom of a man illumines his face,
    And the coarseness of his countenance is changed."

At the end of the ninth chapter, a series of such
sayings is inserted which carries us over into the
tenth chapter. They are suggested by Koheleth's
argument that wisdom is better than strength,
even though the wise man be poor and his words
be not heeded. The commentator cannot resist
the temptation to add (ix. 17-x, 3):

(*a*) "The words of the wise, though spoken quietly, are
    better than the loud cry of an arch-fool."
(*b*) "Better is wisdom than weapons."
(*c*) "A dead fly spoils the perfumer's precious oil."[51]
(*d*) "A little foolishness annuls wisdom."
(*e*) "A wise man's mind is on his right side,
    but a fool's mind is on his left."
(*f*) "When a fool struts in his senseless way,
    he says of everyone else 'he is a fool.'"

In this same chapter, we encounter another
series of no less than nine sayings (x. 8-15), entirely in the style of the Book of Proverbs, some
dealing with wisdom, others with what one might
call practical advice of a somewhat philistine
character.[52] The sayings so manifestly interrupt

---

[51] To suggest that a fool can vitiate the constructive activity of a
wise man.
[52] They will be found grouped together in the Appendix.

the context that, unless we remove them altogether, we cannot follow the argument of Koheleth, which is concerned with the vanity to be found in govermental affairs. There is another insertion of the same character at the end of the chapter (x. 18)

> "Through neglect, the beamwork sinks,
> And through idleness, the house leaks."

likewise in no connection with what precedes or follows.

In addition, someone, anxious to inculcate moderation in feasting, incidental to the contrast set forth by Koheleth between proper merriment and riotous living adds:

"A feast is made for laughter,
  With wine to enliven life,
  and [sufficient] money to provide for everything." (x. 19.)

As a result, only seven of the twenty verses of this chapter form part of the original text—an illustration of the extent to which the book of Koheleth was subject to enlargement and modification, in the desire to make it conform to the traditional picture and to the teachings of a virtuous and wise king, who was supposed to be the author.

Once more we encounter practical advice in the eleventh chapter (xi. 3-4)

(*a*) "If the clouds be filled with rain,
        they will empty themselves on earth."
(*b*) "If a tree falls to the south, or to the north, where the
        tree falls, there it remains."
(*c*) "A wind observer does not sow,
        And a cloud gazer does not harvest."

The similarity of these sayings with those in the tenth chapter (8-15 and 18) suggests that they are extracts from one and the same collection, whereas in chapters seven and eight and in the appendix to the book (xii. 9-14) in which miscellaneous comments and reflections are introduced,[53] the "maxim" commentator appears to draw from a collection of sayings, dealing primarily with the aspects of wisdom, and of which the last quotation:

"The words of the wise are as goads,
And collections are as nails driven with a mace" (xii. 11)

may represent either the introduction or the colophon.

The maxims are thus of two kinds, vacillating between practical advice and the praise of wisdom, and extracted, perhaps, from two collections, though there is no inherent reason why one collection should not have contained both kinds of sayings.

## XI

## THE POPULARITY OF KOHELETH

We have thus succeeded in separating from the original text two distinct classes of additions, one series in illustration of the traditional Solomon as the pious and God-fearing king, the other showing Solomon as the wise king. Through these two classes of insertions the picture of Solomon as the reputed author of the book is made to conform to that of the Solomon of tradition. What is of even

---

[53] See the comments on these verses p. 240 *et seq.*

greater import, the effect of the teachings in the genuine and original portions of the book is counteracted by the pious reflections and by good orthodox maxims inculcating wisdom, caution, the exercise of practical judgment, of moderation and the practice of other conservative and "safe" virtues. The book of Koheleth was thus given the stamp of orthodoxy, and with this stamp could without risk be included in a sacred collection.

We have still to consider a pertinent question that might be raised at this point. Why did pious commentators and collectors of sayings occupy themselves at all with the book? If Koheleth's teachings were objectionable or heretical, why was the book not suppressed or allowed to die a natural death by being left severely alone? Why did its opponents decide to advertise the book by attacking it? The answer is that Koheleth at the time of its appearance must have aroused too much comment to be ignored. It could not be suppressed because it became too popular, just as the popular traditions about Creation, about the Deluge, and about the patriarchal days, circulating among the people, could not be suppressed, and were therefore embodied by pious writers, who gave to the tales an interpretation in the spirit of the teachings of the Hebrew prophets.

The book of Koheleth belongs, as we have seen, to the age when an author was associated with a production, to the extent that a writer would be tempted to trade on the prominence acquired by a figure of the past, embellished by legend and tradition, so as to secure a wider hearing for what he had to say. The device of the author of our book to pass himself off under the *nom de plume* of Koheleth as Solomon must have created for his production something that corresponded to a "mild sensation" in our days. The device must have had an effect to be compared to a "headliner" in a modern newspaper, announcing to its readers: "Discovery of a lost Work of King Solomon. Old Wiseacre says that 'All is Vanity.'" Add to this the novelty of the point of view from which Koheleth treated the activities and experiences of life, its breezy and unconventional tone, its bold attack upon the conventional beliefs of the day, its exposure of the foibles of men and of the evils of his times, and we have a combination that gave to the book an irresistible charm which must have affected even those to whom the teachings were distasteful. At all events, Koheleth aroused a popularity that made it difficult if not impossible for those who opposed the book to suppress its fascinating and dangerous philosophy. Orthodox circles therefore, finding it impossible to kill the book, began to busy themselves with the endeavor to give a different turn to Koheleth's arguments by insertions that would tone down the skeptical implications. Accordingly, they proceeded to touch up the portrait of the king here and there so as to make his features conform to the Solomon of Jewish orthodoxy. With pious comments, urging the fear of God, and by emphasizing the rewards that follow upon virtue and the punishment for wrong doing, Koheleth was actually transformed into a pious king, and by means of wise saws, setting forth the advantages of wisdom and offering practical and sober advice for the guidance of life, the face of the wise Solomon was superimposed on the now blurred features of the original Koheleth.

But even these two classes of additions, extensive as they are, and sufficient to conceal entirely the true nature of the teachings of the book, do not exhaust the modifications which Koheleth in the course of time underwent. In order to make the book still more palatable, the thought of Koheleth was elaborated by shorter or longer additions, and by explanatory comments, generally with a further view of diverting attention from the *real* Koheleth, whose conclusions, even when not specifically stated, do not accord with these additions and comments. Perhaps the most notable instance of such an elaboration of Koheleth's thought, but which also takes off its sharp edge, is to be found in the third chapter where after the author has announced that "Everything has its appointed time and there is a time [determined] for every occurrence under the sun" and has illustrated this by adding

"There is a time [appointed] to be born, and a time to die. There is a time [appointed] for planting, and a time for uprooting,"

someone has added a series of no less than twelve other antitheses.[54]  Now, apart from the inartistic

[54] Given in full in the commentary, p. 210, and in the Appendix, p. 249.

89

heaping up of illustrations of which a skillful writer like Koheleth would not be guilty, and apart from the repetitions in the list itself,[55] their extraneous character is revealed by their deviation from the point which Koheleth wishes to impress upon us. He is not interested in a trivial attempt to enumerate the contrasts presented by the experiences of life, but in showing that everything is foreordained to happen at the time fixed for it. This is made evident by the question which Koheleth poses (v. 9)—what is the use of all one's work, since what is to happen is bound to happen and to take place, moreover, at the very time that God has determined for it? The time of birth is fixed, as is the time of death. It is foreordained and not dependent upon man's will or pleasure when one should plant, just as the uprooting, referring either to the pulling up of the fruit that has ripened beneath the soil, or perhaps to the destruction through a storm or blight of what has been planted, is determined by God. When, however, to these two apt illustrations, emphasizing that the beginning and the end of things—and by implication also what lies between—are predetermined, irrespective of anything that man may do, there is added a long series of antitheses that merely represent contrasts,

"A time to destroy, and a time to repair,
A time to break down, and a time to build up,
A time to weep and a time to laugh," etc., etc., ending with
"A time of war, and a time of peace,"

---

[55] See the comments to iii. 3–8.

the supplement gives an entirely different turn to
the chapter, as though Koheleth had intended to
suggest the commonplace notion of "everything
in its season," that there is a proper time to destroy
and an appropriate time to repair, a proper moment
for pulling a building down and a proper occasion
to rebuild it, a time when war should be declared
and a time when peace ought to be made, and the
like. What Koheleth has in mind is to set forth the
doctrine of predestination, which, though following
logically from the conception of a power in abso-
lute control of the universe, was regarded as most
unorthodox, since it seemed to deprive man of
independent initiative, and left no place for the
exercise of Divine justice in punishing the evil-
doers and in rewarding the virtuous. The commentator or the several hands that added the long
series of antitheses did so with the intent of
removing from the chapter the implication that
the world is ruled by blind fate. So successful was
the device that most of the modern exegetes have
interpreted Koheleth's thought as showing that
everything has its proper time—thus missing the
entire point of the real argument, which leads
logically to the question (in verse 9) as to the futility of all human effort.

Another addition of this nature, intended again
to take off the edge of Koheleth's gentle cynicism,
occurs in the fourth chapter, in which he argues
that toil without enjoyment is particularly foolish
when one is all alone, unmarried or without a

business partner to whom one might become attached. For whom under such circumstances,
asks Koheleth pertinently, does one work and deprive oneself of the joy of life? (iv. 8.) It is an un-
comfortable question to be put to a philistine steeped
in the conventionalities of the world about him,
which proclaims with smug satisfaction that honest
toil is essential to the well-being of men; and so he
purposely misunderstands the kernel of Koheleth's
philosophy and tries to make us believe that Koheleth was merely railing against single blessedness—
against existence without a partner in life or in
business. Our conventional moralist gives an entirely different turn to the question which Koheleth
puts by holding up in sober fashion (iv. 9-12) the
advantages of partnership over the man who stands
alone,

> "Two are better than one,
> for they secure a better return for their toil.
> In case they fall, the one can lift his fellow up,
> but if a single person falls there is none to lift him
> up." (iv. 9-10.)

Very sound advice to the one who wishes to go
into mercantile life, that he should take a partner so
as to be able to do a larger amount of business, and
in case of failure to be in a better position to get on
his feet again—but, surely, that is not the kind of
practical wisdom which Koheleth had in mind. Our
moralist adds, with a suggestion of the advantages
of conjugal partnership,

> "If two sleep together, they get warm,
> but how can a single person get warm?" (iv. 11.)

And in order to take us still further away from Koheleth's question he urges that in case of an attack, two have a better chance of standing against one, and that in such a three-cornered fight a draw is the worst that can happen.

"If some one attacks, there are two to withstand,
  And a triple cord is not easily snapped." (iv. 12.)

Therefore, get married, so as to have someone to work for, and take a business partner so as to stimulate your toil, whereas what Koheleth wants to impress on us is that a life of toil, even though one has a hundred children (vi. 3), is foolish without enjoyment. Why work in order to leave one's fortune to someone who has not toiled for it (ii. 21)?

We have already called attention to little comments in which the style of Koheleth is consciously imitated,[56] so as to strengthen the impression that our author is *really* orthodox and only appears to argue on the other side so as to make the orthodox answer all the more effective. By the side of such comments, we have others which are intended to give a serious turn to what was set forth by Koheleth in an ironical spirit.

Koheleth tells us (viii. 2-3) to be careful in dealing with a king. Do what he commands, instead of rushing to him to complain, for a king will always do what he pleases. No one can ask a king "What art thou doing?" By means of a small comment, "because of the oath of God" (inserted

---

[56] *e.g.*, iii. 17. See above, p. 75.

at the close of verse 2), the impression is conveyed that Koheleth advises one to obey the king because one has sworn allegiance to him in God's name. Similarly, by adding to Koheleth's caution against lodging a complaint with a king, because it is useless, a small comment, "do not plead a bad cause" (inserted at the close of verse 3), the irony of the advice is lost, and an entirely different impression conveyed from the one which Koheleth had in mind.

## XII

### APOLOGIZING FOR KOHELETH

Despite all these additions, calculated to amend the character of the book, to convert its skepticism and cynicism into orthodoxy and conventional morality, to make it appear that the author was virtuous and God-fearing and that, appearances to the contrary, the entire aim of the book was to put together a series of maxims for the guidance of life of the same general character as the Book of Proverbs—despite all this, a doubt must have remained in the minds of the orthodox manipulators whether they had *wholly* succeeded in their aim, for at the close of the book a number of statements are added the apologetic character of some of which is unmistakable. We have already considered two which are due to the "pious" and "maxim" commentators.[57] Besides these, there are three others the purpose of which is to assure the reader that Koheleth aimed to be a

[57] See above, p. 73 and p. 86.

real teacher, and that if some things in the book
appeared strange and bold, one must remember
that he was frank and that after all books must
not be taken too seriously, for an author writes
because it gives him pleasure to do so. We must
assume that each of these additions was made
separately, and that taken together they represent
somewhat varying opinions about Koheleth, though
all are conceived in a more or less apologetic spirit.
The first addition (xii. 9), after stating that Koheleth made other collections of proverbs,[58] and thus
implying the identity of Koheleth with Solomon,
as a compiler of proverbs, reads

"Furthermore, Koheleth was a wise man and in other ways
taught people, compiling and searching."

He is, therefore, a safe guide to follow. One must
not suspect his orthodoxy, but the very emphasis
placed on the assurance that he is "all right,"
shows that some persons continued to shake their
heads. A second hand found it necessary to distinguish between what he wrote and the style in
which he wrote.

"Koheleth aimed at a pleasant style with straightforward
expression." (Verse 10.)

The phrase which conveys the idea of Koheleth's
being frank is somewhat vague—and no doubt
intentionally so—and therefore someone, who

---

[58] In agreement with the Solomonic tradition, I Kings v. 12, and
which shows again incidentally that this addition to Koheleth was made
*after* the completion of our Book of Proverbs, to which it no doubt refers.

perhaps did not approve of thus apologizing for
Koheleth and who felt that the book could stand
on its own merits, added "he spoke the truth."
It must remain, of course, an open question whether
the one who made this addition sympathized
with Koheleth in its original form, or whether he
felt sufficient confidence in the changes that had
been made to give the book a different character,
so as to assure the reader that one is perfectly safe
in looking upon the book as conveying "the truth,"
without any attempt at merely fine writing. Most
interesting of all is the third addition, again in
conscious imitation of the style of Koheleth,[59] so
as to strengthen the impression of authenticity.

"Furthermore, my son, beware of the writing of many
　　books without end
And much discussion [?] [60] is a weariness of the flesh."

The purpose is clearly to suggest to those who
might have some lingering doubts as to the orthodoxy of Koheleth even in its final and entirely
modified form, that after all a book is *only* a book.
The written word must not be regarded as having
the same value as the spoken one, for a man speaks
when he has something to say, whereas a man
may write because he is anxious to say something.
There are so many books in the world, presenting
the same subject from different points of view, that

---

[59] As above, p. 75.
[60] The exact meaning of the term which occurs only in this passage
is not certain. It is generally rendered "study" or "devotion to study."
The parallelism with "writing" suggests rather the meaning "talk," or
"discussion."

they surely cannot all be right. Therefore—do not take books too seriously, and be careful before you decide to add another to the endless list. If you find some things in Koheleth that still impress you as novel and not in accord with the teachings of the old-time religion which was good enough for your parents and ought to be good enough for you, remember that Koheleth was *only*—an author, impelled by the literary impulse to do what you should avoid doing, adding another book to the many that already burden mankind. Also, do not indulge in too much talk, for it leads nowhere and merely wears one out. Koheleth, to be sure, might have approved of such a sentiment, but that would merely prove that the cynic and the advocate of the *status quo* occasionally meet.

" *Duo quum faciunt idem, non est idem.*"

The reflection against the foolishness of too much talk in Koheleth's mouth would have had the usual touch of irony, whereas to the commentator who added it it was a thought to be taken most seriously. If Koheleth had wished to give expression to the sentiment he would have found a place for it in the body of the book. Its position after the final verdict,"all is vanity," which is clearly the end of the book, shows that it is an addition, as also that it is to be taken in a serious spirit, as a further warning against attaching too much importance to mere writing and discussion. The thing to do is, as the pious commentator tells us, "Fear

God and keep his commandments." Read Koheleth if you will, and if you are not fully convinced of Koheleth's orthodoxy, don't enter into further arguments, but follow the dictates of the established religion. Cast your doubts to the wind and "fear God."

We are fortunate in having the actual proof that despite all attempts to alter the tone and character of the book, its orthodoxy continued to be open to suspicion a century before the book was admitted into the canon. The vast compilation of discussions on the Jewish laws and ceremonialism that took place in the schools of the Rabbis in Babylonia and Palestine and known as the Talmud[61] contains a discussion[62] between the schools of Hillel and Shammai—two Rabbis who flourished in the generation before Jesus—in regard to the book of Koheleth. The Shammai school objected to the book as not sacred because in advocating (xi. 9) that one should follow "the inclinations of one's mind and the sight of one's eyes," it contradicted the caution expressed in Numbers xv. 39, "Seek not after your heart and your eyes"; but the Hillel school pointed to the frequent injunction, *e.g.*, v. 6 and xii. 13 to "fear God" as proof of the piety of the author. It is interesting to note that those who opposed the canonization of the book quoted *genuine* passages, whereas the proofs for the other side rested upon the *additions* that

---

[61] See for a general view of the Talmud, the monographs by Emanuel Deutsch and Arsène Darmesteter, published by the American Jewish Publication Society.

[62] Talmud Babli., Sabbath 30 a–b and Megillah 7 a.

were made with the very aim of counteracting the objectionable teachings. The discussion in the Talmud is of value to us in proving that, in the century before this era, all the additions had been made and that in this uncritical age the superimposed parts were looked upon as genuine. The book was regarded as a unit, every word of which as it stands was supposed to have been written by Solomon. The contradictions in the book, however, were so glaring that even pious Rabbis could not close their eyes to them, but it was regarded as sufficient to counterbalance the unorthodox utterances by the pious reflections that had been superimposed. Another indication that the consciences of the pious were not fully convinced of the orthodox character of the book is to be found in the attempts to give a symbolical interpretation to Koheleth. The theological exegetes did not go so far as in the case of the Song of Songs, the secular character of which was too obvious to be overlooked, and which could only be accepted as sacred by being regarded as an allegory with the Beloved viewed as Israel and the lover as Yahweh—but in the Aramaic text of Koheleth, which is a paraphrase rather than a translation, we find the tendency throughout to give to the worldly advice of Koheleth a symbolical and semi-mystical interpretation. "Eat, drink and be merry," becomes a command to rejoice in the law of God and to walk in his ways. The wine is interpreted as the mystic drink hidden in the

Garden of Eden of which man was deprived by his disobedience. The food is the charity to be given to the poor. "Looking upon good," which to Koheleth means "having a good time," becomes an injunction to show one's soul as good and pure before men, to walk in the right path as the means of securing a good reward for one's labors. In the course of this transformation of the book into an allegory, teaching obedience to God's commands, all references to worldly pleasures become a disguise for spiritual joys, cynical reflections on the vanity of life become invitations to seek the salvation of the soul, and even denunciations of injustice in the world are given a semi-mystical interpretation. The symbolism is carried through to the last chapter which instead of being regarded as an impressive and original description of the coming of old age is interpreted as an allegorical picture of Israel's history.[63] The days of youth which Koheleth says are made for enjoyment are the days of Israel's prosperity, while the evil days by which Koheleth means old age and death symbolize the period of the Babylonian Exile; and so throughout the chapter. All this shows that even after the canon of the Old Testament had been fixed and the Book of Koheleth had been accepted as sacred, a lingering doubt remained as to its orthodoxy which could only be dispelled

---

[63] So in the Introduction to the Midrash (*i.e.*, the Rabbinical homily) on the Book of Lamentations. This Midrash also records the attempt to set the book aside because it contained utterances bordering on heresy. ("Midrash Koheleth" to i. 3 and to xi. 9.)

by the application of the allegorical method, such
as a writer like Philo, the Jewish philosopher of
Alexandria who flourished about the time of Jesus,
applied to the entire Old Testament. By such a
method, it was evident, all the strange teachings
of a supposedly sacred book could be given an
interpretation in accord with the strictest orthodoxy. The book was thus saved for the Jewish
and Christian church but, as we have seen, at
the expense of a complete transformation of its
real teachings. Every step that was taken in the
direction of making it worthy of a place in a
sacred collection of orthodox writings was also a
step away from the correct interpretation of
Koheleth's thought. For all that, we should be
grateful to the many hands which manipulated the
book in the interests of Jewish orthodoxy, as also for
the success of their efforts, for without this successful distortion of the book it would in all probability
have been entirely lost, as no doubt other productions were lost, and the world would have been the
poorer for a piece of literature that it could ill afford
to spare. Koheleth is the most fascinating book in
the Old Testament, as the Book of Job is the most
profound, and the Song of Songs the most charming.

## XIII

### TWO QUESTIONS REGARDING KOHELETH

Two questions may be raised by readers, especially by such as have been accustomed to look
upon the book of Koheleth as a unit, and to whom

this historical and critical manner of treating books of a sacred collection may be somewhat novel and possibly startling. These must now be considered. Is it really necessary to assume that the "additions" to the kernel of the book, as above set forth, were made by someone other than the author, and secondly, if we accept the implications of the critical method in studying Biblical books what becomes of their supposedly sacred character? How can Koheleth be regarded as part of a sacred canon?

There are critical scholars who, while recognizing that the book in its present form contains contradictory statements and that it is loaded with maxims not relevant to the main thought of the author, yet maintain the unity of the book[64] on the ground that the additions were made by Koheleth himself for fear of arousing opposition to the book and in order to conceal its real nature as much as possible. Such an assumption would reflect little credit on Koheleth's character. It would stamp him as a hypocrite, in addition to being a coward. The hypocrisy in this instance would have been quite superfluous, since the adoption of a *nom de plume* would have been a sufficient safeguard against any possible attacks of a personal character. It is gratuitous to assume that Koheleth was such a great coward as to surround himself with a double rampart. Moreover, is it likely that a

---

[64] So, *e.g.*, Professor D. S. Margoliouth, of Oxford, in his introduction to *Ecclesiastes*, in the "Temple Bible."

writer who speaks as frankly as Koheleth does, would have conceived the Machiavellian device of himself adding the antidote to the poison that he instils into the minds of his readers? Hardly. A man who is frank is rarely subtle—certainly not subtle enough to appear to be dishonest. Finally in supposing that Koheleth wrote his book in such a way as to disguise his real meaning, we are projecting modern methods of book publication into a period in which books were not published at all in our sense of the word.

We must picture to ourselves Koheleth as a member of a *circle*, interested in the problems with which the book deals. He gives expressions to certain views which he shares with others. What he wrote was spread within a limited range of readers, and if it attracted also the attention of those whose viewpoint was totally different, it was due to the circumstance that the circle to which Koheleth belonged and of which he was in a sense the mouthpiece had acquired sufficient prominence to arouse the opposition of the ortho- dox and pious. In the third century before this era—and even before that—the intellectual life among the Jews was sufficiently advanced to have produced varying shades of opinion on religious matters, as on questions of religious practice. We miss the whole point of Koheleth's philosophy of life, unless we regard it as one outcome among others of considerable independent speculation within the intellectual circles of the period in which

Koheleth flourished. If, belonging to a circle which raised the question as to the basis and sufficiency of the current religious views, Koheleth felt impelled to write at all, the impulse could only have led him to express his point of view—not to conceal it by a clumsy as well as a dishonest trick.

But, it may further be argued, Koheleth may have been a man of many moods. In one of his moods, he may have been a pessimist, perhaps under the influence of a spell of indigestion, in another he may have been optimistically inclined, perhaps because of some pleasant experience. There are other instances of writers who now appear to be skeptics, while at another time what they write bears the earmarks of a reverent believer. Consistency is a rare virtue—even among modern thinkers. It is not easy to say exactly what an elusive writer like Anatole France believes or does not believe. Renan is reported to have said of himself that he did not feel entirely happy unless he contradicted himself twice a day. Who is so chameleon-like in his thought as Bernard Shaw? Reading him is like playing a game of now you see it, now you don't. And Bernard Shaw is a jewel of consistency compared to Gilbert Chesterton whose *métier* it is to be paradoxical, and of whom the only thing certain is that he is uncertain. May not Koheleth have been of this type? Possibly, though in granting this we are again in danger of projecting a modern spirit into an ancient writer.

Now if Koheleth had written two books, we

might even grant the possibility that the one might be orthodox, and the other heterodox, but unfortunately he wrote only one, or at least only one has come down to us; and it is putting too great a strain on one's credulity to ask us to believe, in order to maintain the unity of the book in its present form, that Koheleth was so moody— or rather so silly—as to blow hot and cold at the same time. A man of such mental caliber would hardly have produced anything that could have stood the test of time as Koheleth has done.

Is it reasonable to assume that even the most capricious writer would spoil his own work—and a short book at that—by representing himself as his own opponent? Koheleth, as will be pointed out, is not always consistent. He claims in one paragraph to hate life (ii. 17) and yet elsewhere— and indeed in general—he loves life for life's sake; and though he believes that things in this world are preordained, he does not carry this view to its logical conclusion to the denial of free initiative on the part of man. This, however, is quite a different matter from complaining in one place (viii. 10) that the wicked are honored in life and even after death, and then adding (viii. 11-13) that though sentence may be deferred for evil-doers, yet "it shall not be well with them" and that those who fear God will be prosperous, although elsewhere his plaint is that virtue is not rewarded (vii. 15; ix. 15). The contradictions of which Koheleth in its present form is full affect the main thesis of the entire book, to wit, that because one cannot see the workings of justice in this world, and man can neither understand the present nor know what is going to happen in a world which appears to be ruled by blind chance, the only thing to do is to try to have as good a time as possible. Life without joy is a failure. That is the reflection which, like a refrain, is constantly suggested as Koheleth unfolds his picture of the world in which we live. A writer of many moods might at different times present various *aspects* of a situation, but it is inconceivable that he should upset his *entire* theory of life, just after he has scored a strong point in favor of it. The contradictions in Koheleth are always encountered at a critical point in the exposition of the theme; they come after Koheleth has given utterance to a point of view, particularly startling and obnoxious to the pious and conventional reader. By virtue of this, these contradictory statements reveal themselves as additions made by some *opponent* of Koheleth, who is bent upon controverting him, and who is anxious to set up against Koheleth's unorthodox thoughts the position taken by the pious. Moreover, the style in which most of the additions are written plainly shows that we are dealing with a different writer. Note as an example the prosy and didactic way in which the attempt is made to show that the wicked are punished and the good rewarded in the illustration above given (viii. 11-13), as against the pithy, vigorous and picturesque manner in which

Koheleth sets forth his cynical position that the wicked flourish and are praised after their death in the very place in which they carried on their wicked careers.

Koheleth advises the young to enjoy themselves in every possible way, to follow their inclinations and "put away all trouble from their minds" (xi. 10). Is it conceivable that he would follow this up immediately by advising the same youth "to remove evil from thy flesh?" The one piece of advice is in accord with Koheleth's view of life as unfolded in his book, the other is clearly the warning of one who is concerned for man's spiritual and moral welfare. Chasing away cares so as to enjoy life to the full is the direct opposite of keeping oneself free from sin. Such a contradiction is fundamental and cannot be accounted for by assuming that Koheleth was of a changeable mood. Caprice cannot be carried to the point of illogical absurdity; and this is what we are led to by the attempt to save the unity of the book on the assumption that Koheleth had no real message to convey, and therefore acted the part of the literary buffoon. Not only that, but after ruining his work by making it unintelligible and nonsensical, he proceeded to pad it with illustrations and with maxims of all kinds that interrupt the context and that have no direct bearing either on the author's theme, or on the arguments introduced by him in defense of that theme. Many of these maxims are, to be sure, striking and some are admirable—especially those introduced into Chapters vii, x and xi—but they become much more attractive when put together[65] and regarded as extracts from a collection, than in their present interspersed position in Koheleth, where they are distinctly disturbing to the sequence of the thought which Koheleth wishes to convey to his readers. And again, the style of these sayings differs from that of the body of the book and thus reveals their character as supplements to the real Koheleth, added at some time after the completion of the book. If we had only a few of such sayings, we *might* assume that Koheleth is introducing them as apt quotations, but their large number precludes the reasonableness of such an inartistic procedure on the part of a skillful writer.

## XIV

### BELIEF IN THE BIBLE NOT AFFECTED BY HISTORICAL AND LITERARY CRITICISM

Turning now to the second question—what becomes of the supposedly sacred character of Koheleth and indeed of all the books of the Old and New Testaments, if we treat the books in the manner proposed by the critics? The question is a pertinent one, but the implication that by applying a historical and critical method to the study of the Old and New Testaments, the character of the books as part of a sacred canon is endangered, rests upon an erroneous assumption of the nature of historical criticism. The new approach

---

[65] As has been done in the Appendix p. 249 *et seq.*

towards the books of the Bible which has become a commonplace in modern scholarship throughout the world affects beliefs *about* the Bible, but not belief *in* the Bible. Acceptance of the ascertained results of modern Biblical study obliges us to abandon traditional views held concerning the origin and composition of the books of the Old and New Testaments when these views are shown to be in direct contradiction to facts ascertained as the result of research. This does not mean that the factor of tradition is to be rejected entirely in the critical study. Far from it. A tradition is seldom entirely astray.[66] It rests generally on a basis which has some substantiality, though not necessarily the one assumed by the tradition itself. Besides, it is part of the critical method even when it rejects a tradition to account for its rise, and in doing so criticism generally comes to recognize a residuum of value in the tradition, albeit rejected as a whole. So, *e.g.*, modern study has shown that there are several distinct codes of the Pentateuch, that these codes date from various periods, and that they received their present form as the result of a process of compilation and editing stretching over centuries and terminating not earlier than the end of the fifth century B.C., that is to say, at least seven centuries after the death of Moses to whom tradition ascribed all the laws. While historical

---

[66] For a more detailed discussion of the relationship of Biblical tradition to criticism, see the author's paper on "Constructive Elements in the Critical Study of the Old Testament" (Presidential address, published in the *Journal of Biblical Literature*, volume 36, pp. 1–30).

criticism thus rejects the tradition of the Mosaic origin of the Pentateuchal codes, it yet recognizes the value of the tradition, which would not have arisen had not Moses impressed himself upon his age as a law-giver in the ancient sense of rendering decisions in the name of a deity. Law everywhere in antiquity is carried back to a divine origin, and the tradition which represents Moses as receiving the law from Yahweh, though the form of this tradition in the Pentateuch itself is late, rests upon an early and widespread belief, which thus aims to account for the sanctity attaching to the laws. Furthermore, it is of the essence of law codes to embody very old elements by the side of later decisions and of amendments to original and very ancient decisions. In all the codes to be distinguished in the Pentateuch we come across such old elements; and when we find decisions and statutes that correspond to the social and religious conditions prevailing in the days of Moses, we are justified in attributing them to the great leader under whose stimulus the tribes of Israel are welded into some kind of a unity that marks the beginning of the national life.

Now, it is evident that the critical method, besides in this way utilizing the substantial basis of a tradition which in its complete form it rejects, does not affect the question as to the value of the codes nor of the beliefs which are embodied in them. The test of these beliefs lies outside the scope of historical criticism; it falls within the domain of theology with which historical criticism is in no way concerned.

What applies to the codes of the Pentateuch holds good also for the narratives within which the codes are encased. Historical criticism differentiates these narratives into their component parts. Some of them rest upon a foundation of myth, others represent the outcome of early non-mythical speculation on the mysteries of the universe and of human life. Some of the tales in Genesis and Exodus are folk-tales, reflecting in part conditions of life under patriarchal conditions, and in part representing popular traditions with an historical substratum. The religious value of these narratives resides not in the stories themselves, but in the manner in which the tales are utilized by the compilers and editors to whose combined labors the final form is due, to illustrate certain conceptions of God as the single Power behind and above the universe, and certain ethical principles bearing on the position of man in the universe, or on his duties and obligations. In short, the attitude towards life, illustrated by the codes and the narratives, gives us the *religious* import of the Pentateuch; and the value and underlying truth of this attitude are again entirely independent of the postulates of historical criticism.

This being clearly grasped, it will not seem unreasonable to claim that through the historical background, gained by the application of the critical method to the study of the books of the Bible, we reach a deeper and far keener appreciation of the contents of these books. How much more does the utterance of a prophet—spoken or written— mean to us when we are able to reconstruct the conditions under which the utterance was made? And if, as a result of the new approach towards the Bible, we are led to reject the tradition which places an utterance in the mouth of Isaiah, because it belongs to a period subsequent to that prophet's day, is there not more than a corresponding gain to be recognized in placing the utterance itself in its proper perspective ? Once more, the warning is in place not to confuse the circumstances under which a prophet spoke or wrote with the beliefs upon which his utterances rest, or which they embody. The test of these beliefs, likewise, lies outside of the scope of historical criticism. The same applies to the Psalms, as the most perfect expression of faith in the guidance of a Power conceived in the most sublime spiritual terms. Clearly, the justification of this faith, as well as the capability that the remarkable collection still possesses after the lapse of two milleniums of influencing human lives, is independent of the origin and method of their composition. On the contrary, knowledge of their origin can only help to deepen the impression that they make. The rejection of the tradition about the Psalms may be painful when it is first forced home upon us, because in the course of time the tradition has become so closely bound up with the compositions, themselves, but a moment's reflection must also make it clear that the value of the Psalms has nothing to do with the tradition. What matters it who wrote them or when they were written? Their value is not affected by the answer to such questions, any more than the value of the religious truths and aspirations to which they give such sublime expression.

## XV

### THE OLD TESTAMENT CANON AS A MIRROR OF VARIOUS ASPECTS OF LIFE

Coming back to the Book of Koheleth, it should be borne in mind that the Old Testament gives us the remains of the literature produced by the ancient Hebrews during the eight or possibly nine centuries before this era. Much more was produced than has come down to us, and we know the names at least of some compositions which were lost, because they were *not* preserved as part of a sacred canon. Now the literary life of a people presents many aspects, and we should, therefore, expect to find in the canon traces of all kinds of currents and countercurrents crisscrossing through the ages. Koheleth, the Book of Job, the Song of Songs, Proverbs, Ruth, and Daniel represent some of these currents, all bound up with the religious and social interests of the people among whom these books arise. These productions, of an entirely different character from the laws, the early narratives, the historical books and the collections of the prophets, touch life at many angles. Their inclusion in the canon is due to the impression which they made and to the influence which they must have exerted, although we are no longer able to trace the course of this influence in detail. The anonymity of all these productions, the reasons for which I have tried to set forth, was a factor in making them the expression of currents and countercurrents in the life of the people as a whole, with far less regard for individual points of view (which, to be sure, are also to be recognized in them) than we are apt to associate with a modern literary product. Anonymity, leading by a natural transition to collective authorship, gives to such books more particularly, as Koheleth and the Book of Job, the character of "Tracts of the Times," voicing views held in certain circles. These views formed a part of the intellectual life of the people, as much as did the expression of religious aspirations in the Psalms, and as the Song of Songs, a collection of popular love ditties, reflects another aspect of the life and emotions of the people. It was proper, therefore, that in a collection which aimed to preserve what was *best* in the literary legacy of the past, and which had made its way into the thought of the people, literary productions less distinctively religious and bordering on the secular should have found a place, by the side of books that were in a superlative degree religious. Religion among ancient peoples —and particularly among a people like the Hebrews passing through such a remarkable religious experience—touches life at so many points and connects with so many avenues that themes dealing with problems of life and popular customs that for us would be purely secular take on a religious aspect. The dividing line between religious and what we should regard as secular literature is not so sharply drawn under conditions prevailing in antiquity. From the modern point of view such productions as Koheleth, Book of Job, Proverbs, and Song of Songs are distinctly secular, and in order to be grasped in their real meaning should so be regarded; but they all—and particularly the first three— are branches of the main religious current, running through the life of the ancient Hebrews. This trait was recognized or instinctively felt by those who were instrumental in bringing together the canon of the best literature of the past, and therefore the books in question were included in a category from which in a stricter sense, as not being sacred in their contents, they should have been excluded. The difference of degree in sacredness between these books and the first two divisions of the Old Testament—the Pentateuch with the historical books Joshua, Samuel and Kings and the Prophets—was admitted by the Jewish Rabbis, but when after considerable discussion, of which we have traces in the Talmud,[67] they were placed in the third division known as "miscellaneous writings," it was all the more impor-

---

[67] The question was raised whether these books "defile the hands"—a peculiar phrase, meaning whether they had to be handled with special care as was the case with the books of the first two divisions of the O. T.

tant to emphasize the sacred character given to them, in order to put them on a par with the books of the other two divisions. This end was acomplished by additions to some of the books—as in the case of Koheleth and Job—and by a religious-allegorical interpretation given to others, as in the case of the Song of Songs.[68]

XVI

## THE ORIGINAL *VERSUS* THE MODIFIED KOHELETH

Confining ourselves here to Koheleth, and leaving the details with regard to Job and Song of Songs for special treatment of these two important and fascinating productions, it is the book in its *present* form, as finally accepted by the Rabbis who fixed the canon, that is sacred—not the original Koheleth which, in fact, was objectionable from the narrower and more exclusive religious point of view. It is not begging the question, but the statement of a fact which may be accepted as literal, that there are *two* books of Koheleth, one expressive of views regarding life held in certain circles, which in an independent spirit had cut loose from the conventional views that had grown up under the influence of the prophets' conception of divine government of the universe, the other book as modified, to make it conform, so far as possible, to the teachings prevalent in orthodox and conservative circles. It is the latter book which was

---

[68] See above, p. 55.

admitted into the canon. The former not only would have been rejected, it *was* rejected by virtue of the additions to which it was subjected, and which gave to the teachings of the real Koheleth an entirely different direction, so different that if the author of the original book were to come back to life, he would have considerable difficulty in recognizing his offspring.

Will it seem to be going too far to claim that we cannot understand the modified Koheleth, without making the endeavor to get back to the original and real Koheleth? I hold not, and that on the contrary Koheleth dressed up in orthodox garb, himself becomes more intelligible to us if we recognize the manner in which he received his strange disguise. By separating the original kernel from the subsequent additions, we are placed in a position to follow the process which resulted in giving us a new book, that could be regarded as worthy of a place in a sacred coltion. Nor need we accuse those who thus changed the entire character of the book of any attempt at willful deception. Apart from the fact that, as we have seen,[69] it was perfectly natural and indeed inevitable before the days when the claims of individual authorship were fully recognized for any piece of writing which conveyed a vital message to be subject to additions and to steady modification, pious commentators, as well as those who supplemented Koheleth's pithy sayings by others

[69] See above, p. 32.

which to them seemed to be relevant, or which
supplemented Koheleth without being relevant,
felt that they were rendering a service to the cause
of religion and of ethics by showing on the one
hand how the questions raised by Koheleth *might*
be answered, and on the other how maxims intended
as a guidance for life could be supplemented by
others. From the critical and modern point of
view we recognize the intent of these additions to
be two-fold, to make the figure of Solomon as the
reputed author of the book conform to the Solomon of orthodox tradition, and to give to the book
the character of being a collection of sayings,
edifying and suitable for general reading like the
Book of Proverbs. We may feel certain that
the manipulators of the original book, living in
an uncritical age which had not developed the
historical sense that to us has become a commonplace, felt that they were improving the
book by furnishing the antidote to Koheleth's
teachings.

To be sure, Koheleth himself was in part to
blame for the production of this new and modified
edition of his book. His device in choosing a *nom
de plume*, which was intended to convey the impression that King Solomon was the author, furnished the opponents of the book with a good
excuse for making the contents of the book conform
to the picture of the idealized Solomon. The very
success of the device thus gave the opponents of
Koheleth a weapon which they used against the

author. If Koheleth *was* Solomon, there was every reason why he should be made to think and write as Solomon, and the only Solomon recognized by an uncritical age was the one that had grown up under the influence of the tradition which instinctively converted all the figures of the past into types of piety and wisdom.

The *sacred* book of Koheleth is therefore the one that appears in our Bibles. That is the one which supplies us with the answer to the doubts raised by the author as to the evidence of a reign of justice in this world. The book in its final form is the one which supplies a goal to life—denied by the original Koheleth. That goal is pithily set forth in one of the supplements at the end of the book and repeated at various places in the additions to the body of the book, "Fear God and keep his commandments." The modified Koheleth is the one who warns us that God will bring man to judgment for his acts. It is Koheleth in an orthodox garb, who assures us that, appearances to the contrary, wickedness is punished and that the world is ruled by a just Providence.

Finally, be it emphasized once more that we should be grateful to those who thus succeeded in giving to Koheleth the form of a book that could be used for religious edification, for without this the book would probably have been lost, as so many other productions which did not find a place in the canon failed to be preserved. The new Koheleth saved the old one.

## XVII

### KOHELETH AND HIS "PHILOSOPHY OF LIFE"

Having set forth the history of the book and its real character, together with the modifications which resulted in producing what is virtually a second Koheleth, converting a secular book into a sacred one, we are now prepared to pass on to an outline of the philosophy of life embodied in the original portions of Koheleth. In doing so I have a two-fold purpose in view, to show that the attitude of the author towards the problems of human existence confirms the conclusion, reached from other considerations, as to the late date of the book, between the close of the third century and the beginning of the second century B.C., and on the other hand to assign to the book its proper place in Palestinian literature, which will incidentally justify its inclusion among the choice productions of the human mind that have a message, not limited to any particular period or clime.

The basic thought of Koheleth, repeated some twenty times, is that "all is vanity" in this world in which we move and have our being. The author proceeds to prove this by taking up one phase of human activity after the other. In this way he makes clear what he means by "vanity," and on what he bases his philosophy of life. His main contention is that there is no real progress in the world, despite continued and uninterrupted activity. In the poetic introduction (i. 3-11) which

may be regarded as a summary of his philosophy,
probably added by the author after he had finished
his work, he sets forth an idea which must have
seemed startling when first uttered, that nature
herself shows the absence of any real aim or
progress in the universe. There is merely endless
repetition. Things are in a state of constant flux,
but there is no advance in nature. The sun moves
from east to west and back again to the east. The
wind shifts from south to north and comes back to
the direction whence it started. The rivers seem to
be rushing towards a goal, but there is no goal, for
they continue forever to flow to the sea into which
they empty their waters, but which is never full.
Nature herself seems to grow weary of this monotonous moving picture, always unwinding the
same reel, and it is natural, therefore, that human
life, which likewise proceeds in a never-ending
circle, should become wearisome. What profit has
man of all of his activity, seeing that one generation after the other passes away, each doing the
same things, each always active and yet none
pushing towards a definite goal? There *is* no goal
to human existence any more than to nature.
That is the true significance of the famous phrase,
coined by Koheleth, that "There is nothing new
under the sun" (i. 9). If there were something
really new, it would be an indication of a real advance towards some goal. The reason why some
things which happen in the world appear to be
new is because what has happened is forgotten.

The record is lost. It is interesting to note, as an illustration of the "modernity" of Koheleth, that this thought of endless repetition in nature, which forms the introduction to his book, is encountered among thinkers of our own days and for whom it likewise forms the starting point of their philosophy. So Amiel in his "Journal Intime" (under date of the 4th of August, 1880) speaks of "nature being governed by continuity, the continuity of repetition * * * profound monotony in universal movement—there is the simplest formula furnished by the spectacle of the world." Similarly Prince Eugène Troubetzkoy, who holds a chair in the University of Moscow, in an article in the *Hibbert Journal* for January, 1918 (page 179), concludes, from the everlasting repetition in nature, as does Koheleth, the absence of a purpose in life. "Life," he says, "is always repeating the same vicious circle." It would appear indeed that Koheleth by his observation of the endless and monotonous repetition in nature has hit upon the real basis of pessimistic philosophy wherever we encounter it—whether in India, or in the West, in the ideas of Schopenhauer, as in those of Nietzsche, concerning the eternal cycle.

Koheleth is, of course, aware of the obvious objection to all this, that whereas nature is constantly repeating herself, and the experiences of life pass along in a circle of endless repetition, yet the repetition is never precisely the same, neither in nature nor in history. No two trees are exactly alike, no human experiences are completely copies of one another. The history of one people differs considerably from that of another. New discoveries are constantly being made that change the aspects of existence. Koheleth's answer would be that the variations in the repetition do not affect essentials, either in nature or in life. In contrast to Amiel who says that in order to avoid *fastidium* through the eternal repetition of nature, we must lay stress "upon the small differences which exist, and then by learning to enjoy repetition," Koheleth would claim that such differences as, *e.g.*, the difference between the course of the sun in summer and its course in winter is a negligible quantity. The sun rises and sets in constant succession—that is the essential fact; and so one generation succeeds another and passes through the same general experiences. The general is the essential, which is not affected by any specific variation, either in the life of individuals or of peoples. Besides, what guarantee have we that even the variations had not occurred endless times in the remote and forgotten past? The individual is constantly forgetting what he once knew. The acquisition of knowledge is counterbalanced by the accompanying process of dropping the contents of one's memory; and so the collective memory of mankind loses by the wayside facts and experiences which later crop up anew. Discovery is rediscovery. Perhaps nature herself shares in this weakness of having forgotten what she did in the past.

Furthermore—and this is the more serious side of Koheleth's thought—the new does not represent a genuine advance over the old. If the aspects of life are changed by the different circumstances under which life is passed, by inventions and by so-called reforms and improvements, what is it, Koheleth would interpose, except looking at life through different pieces of colored glass? Life appears to be different but in reality is not, because there is no nearer approach to any goal. The world is no better than it was in the remote past. Man is not happier. Life continues to be a struggle. Sorrow follows man as a shadow, precisely as it did his forefathers. We see around us the same evils as in the days of yore. We are beset by the same temptations and fall a victim to them. Passions continue to rule, the reign of injustice never comes to an end and wrong remains triumphant. Such are the implications in the general view of the world set forth by Koheleth in the introduction, which like an overture announces the musical theme that is to be set forth in its many variations.

Perhaps the most serious defect in the book from the point of view of literary art is the absence of any system in the development of this theme. The book is more in the nature of a series of *causeries*, passing lightly from one phase of the subject to the other without regard either to logical order or strict consistency. There is no gradual approach to a climax as there is in the unfolding of the central theme in the far more systematically

constructed book of Job, with which Koheleth is
allied. In Job, each aspect of the perplexing and
apparently insoluble problem of the reason for
unjust suffering in a world supposed to be created
by a wise and just God is thoroughly exhausted
before another is taken up. When we reach the
end of the discussion between Job and his friends, [70]
despite the imperfect character of the last series of
speeches, [71] we feel that everything that could be
brought forward has been said. Not so Koheleth,
who is suggestive rather than exhaustive, lighting
up his theme sporadically here and there, but not
illuminating all its angles. The attempts which
have been made by some modern scholars to obtain a better sequence in the unfolding of the
theme by a rearrangement of verses and sections,
on the assumption that in the course of trans-
mission the correct order was lost, [72] must be pronounced failures, because they substitute for the
gentle cynic, who with an ironical smile on his lips
exposes life's vagaries with a delicate touch peculiar-
ly his own, a rather forbidding and pedantic logician,
who mercilessly and in cold blood imposes on his
readers a gloomy system of pessimistic philosophy.

Koheleth is a dilettante in philosophy. He
would refuse to subscribe to any school of thought.

---

[70] At the end of Chapter xxxi, which, as the subscript "End of the
words of Job" shows, was originally the close of the book.

[71] Chapters xxii-xxxi.

[72] The late Professor Bickell, of Vienna, justified his rearrangement on
the view that the string connecting the single leaves of the manuscript which
formed our text broke, with a resultant confusion in the attempt to put the
leaves together again.

He is a free lance and is in turn a pessimist and a *bon vivant*, a sympathizer with human suffering and a belittler of human ambition, but he is always in good humor. He smiles at the world. He is scintillating in his thought, rather than profound. His style is not ponderous, as is the language of Job, but light. He is too full of good humor to be a really great and serious philosopher. He belongs to the type of thinkers whom Renan characterizes as not being altogether happy unless they contradict themselves at least twice a day. Koheleth is not afraid of the charge of inconsistency, but he would have his answer ready, "Why not—life itself is full of inconsistencies." And so, literary artist though he is by the very simplicity and pungency of his style, he is willing to be inartistic when it comes to the unfolding of his theme. He indulges in repetitions, and jumps rapidly, without logical transition, from one aspect of his subject to the other.

To the general refrain that all is vanity, he frequently adds the corollary that life is a game of "chasing after wind"—a most picturesque phrase to illustrate the foolishness of ambition, which is as unsatisfactory as the attempt to catch the wind. Wisdom is chosen as the first illustration to prove that life is an empty bubble. What does one gain by being as wise as Solomon, by acquiring knowledge in excess of anyone else? The ambition itself is a mischievous impulse that God has implanted in the human breast merely to worry and torture man (i. 13), for the more one knows, the unhappier one becomes on recognizing through one's wisdom how unsatisfying are all the fleeting pleasures of this world. When you come to examine them, sport and mirth become synony- mous with folly and madness (ii. 2). The thought in Koheleth's mind seems to be that the man who becomes wise and who attains to real knowledge inevitably recognizes that the pursuit of happiness must end in *ennui*. One grows tired of life, as na- ture becomes tired of everlastingly doing the same things. Monotony in nature is paralleled by *ennui* in human life.

Ah, but perhaps the reason why happiness does not satisfy one is because one does not get enough of it. On the contrary, says Koheleth, the more one gets, the less does it satisfy; and, as an illustration, he sets forth in detail all the possible pleasures that a man could have. Almost reveal- ing his disguise for King Solomon, Koheleth gives a picture of the reign of that king as embellished by legend and extravagant tradition.[73] Solomon arrayed in all his glory is brought before us—the king of superior wisdom and unlimited power, able to command whatever pleased his fancy. The test is complete because, when one can obtain everything, one is in a position to note the net result of satis- fying one's desires to the full. What does Koheleth as king find after building palaces and laying out parks and reservoirs,. after surrounding himself

---

[73] The picture accords with the description of Solomon's wealth, his large retinue and building activities as set forth in I Kings, Chapters ix and x.

with an enormous household with plenty of servants, and with singers and musicians to cater to his pleasure to the full, and after indulging his taste in women? He grows weary. Life does not satisfy him. The monotony of it all tires him, for though every day may bring its own round of pleasures and festivities and homage, the variety is exhausted after a while, and the ever revolving circle begins anew. The refrain "All is vanity and chasing after wind" introduced here (ii. 11) to which Koheleth adds "nothing was worth while" strikes home with special force, because of the completeness of the test, for surely the experiment of life could not be made under more favorable circumstances. No one can get more out of life than a king. The example enables us to specify the vanity of existence as due to two causes, first because there is no goal in all one's activities and pleasures, and secondly because one necessarily grows tired of both after some time. Without a goal, without real progress, life must be empty— and Koheleth is frank enough to assert that it *is* empty. However, he leaves us one consolation— wisdom is better than folly, for through wisdom, which gives light, one at least can see the vanity of it all, whereas folly is darkness. This reservation is characteristic of Koheleth. It emphasizes the gentleness of his cynicism. He retains his good humor, and therefore warns us against the conclusion which would be natural to a morose spirit, that one might as well be foolish as be wise.

No, says Koheleth, do not be so foolish as to suppose that it is better to be mad than to be sane. Keep your sanity so that you may go through life with a clear vision. To be sure, you must not expect any advantage from not being a fool, for the same end meets both the wise and the one who is not wise. Both will be forgotten and the one dies precisely as does the other (ii. 16).

## XVIII

### ANCIENT AND LATER BELIEFS REGARDING THE DEAD

This thought that there is a common fate in store for all—oblivion—is a corollary to the view which declares that life must end in *ennui*. There is no goal to death any more than to life. If death led to anything further, Koheleth's system, so far as he has one, would fall to pieces. He dwells upon this common end to all alike and goes so far as to question (iii. 19-21) whether man's spirit has a destiny superior to that of the beast. Accepting the point of view which is also orthodox doctrine (Genesis iii. 19), that man is of the dust and to dust returns, Koheleth sees no reason why this does not also hold good of animals. So he concludes of man as of beasts that "all go to one place" (iii. 20). Our author thus shares the belief which was common to Semites, that the dead are gathered in the earth. From many sources[74] we know that this gathering place was conceived of as a great cavern

---

[74] See Jastrow, "Hebrew and Babylonian Traditions" p. 197 *et seq.*

in which the dead lie huddled together—conscious but inactive. The contribution that Koheleth makes to the time-honored conception lies in the corollary that man's end is not superior to that in store for the beast. And yet the question which he poses (iii. 21)—"Who knows whether the spirit of the children of men mounts up and the spirit of the beast goes down"—is an indication that the author lived in an age which had passed beyond the primitive conception and had advanced to an attempt to differentiate between the fate in store for the dead. The thought of a heavenly abode for at least some human souls must have been current, or the question would be an idle one. Such an implied differentiation between the fate of those favored of God and that of those who do not secure favor is inherent in the conception of a divine Providence, as set forth by the great prophets of the eighth and succeeding centuries. The essential feature of that conception was, as we have seen, that the national Yahweh differs from other tribal protectors, inasmuch as He rules the world according to standards of justice and, therefore, imposes upon those who claim to be His adherents the obligation to regulate their lives by these standards. It was a logical corollary that a just God punishes wrong and rewards virtue; and this in turn led to an extension of the exercise of divine justice beyond the grave. It was inconceivable that a just God could be so inconsistent as to consign the good and the bad alike to the same fate. To be sure, as long as

Yahweh, though a just God, was tied to national limitations, His concern was mainly for the group and only incidentally for the individual within the group. The prophets of the pre-exilic period are stirred up by the national situation, and have little concern for individuals, except in so far as the distressing political turmoils and the unsatisfactory social conditions, entailing general suffering and affecting all classes of the inhabitants, showed themselves in the lives of individuals. But when, through the lessons learned by the temporary extinction of the national life, the conception of a national Protector, punishing His own people, because they did not measure up to the standards imposed by Him, was logically enlarged to that of the single Power above and behind the phenomena of the universe, the individual fell under the control of a guiding and supervising Providence, equally with the group.

This process of an equalization between the relations of the individual and of the group to the universal Jehovah was one of slow growth, and it is not until close to the threshold of our era that we encounter the definite belief in a reward for the virtuous after death, in contradistinction to the punishment of the wicked. Such a solution offered the only satisfactory answer to the perplexing problem, arising out of the conception of a universal Power of good creating a world for the exercise of justice and the promotion of righteousness. It was the only way in which one could explain the injustice and unmerited suffering so manifest in the world. In the Book of Job, this solution is not brought forward, though suggested in a famous passage[75] that represents a subsequent insertion, and that has in addition been manipulated so as to accord more fully with the later beliefs. By the time, however, that Koheleth was written the logical sequence was drawn—at least in some circles—that the innocent suffering of the pious in this world would be compensated by the assurance of a blessed hereafter; and correspondingly that the wicked would meet their merited punishment in another world, if they successfully escaped their doom in this one. This consideration of itself leads us to place Koheleth *after* Job; he is separated from Job by about a century.

There are some scholars who are inclined to place the author of Koheleth among the Sadducees,[76] because this Jewish sect denied the doctrine of a resurrection of the dead, in contrast to the Pharisees who accepted the belief as a corollary to be drawn from the conception of a just God in control of the fate of mankind. We must not, however, press Koheleth's intimation that there is no difference between the ultimate fate of man and that in store for the beast (iii. 19) too hard, certainly not to the point of making him an

---

[75] Job xix. 25-27. The verses as they stand—particularly v. 26—furnish no sense. The proof of this is to be seen in the lack of agreement among commentators, with each one proposing a solution of his own for the unintelligible—because corrupt—text.

[76] So particularly Ludwig Levy, "Das Buch Qoheleth" (Leipzig, 1912).

adherent of a particular school of thought. He is independent of any school. It is true, however, as we know from other sources, that the Sadducees, as the more conservative as well as the more aristocratic party, clung to the traditional belief in a general gathering place for the dead, while the Pharisees, the sect of the people, were more progressive in yielding to the further development of both religion and practice along the new path mapped out by the prophet's conception of divine government. Personal piety as a means of securing divine power was one of the consequences of the new doctrine. Accordingly, we find the curious contradiction in the Pharisaic party of being on the one hand the advocates of detailed ceremonialism which was a by-product of personal piety, and, on the other hand, more advanced in their religious thought.[77] This involved the acceptance of a radically different view of life after death, making not only a distinction between the fate of the good and that of the wicked, but likewise leading to a doctrine of rewards and punishments, and as a further and logical implication to the unfolding of a doctrine of the resurrection of the dead. These three aspects of life after death follow one another in a natural sequence. The passage in Koheleth is proof that, at the time of the appearance of the book, a special place for the dead in heaven, in contrast to the subterranean cave, formed part of the

[77] For further details of the Pharisees and Sadducees, the reader is referred to Schuerer, "History of the Jewish People in the Time of Jesus Christ," ii, 2, pp. 10-43.

new belief, though again we must be warned against pressing the language too hard.

Koheleth is averse to speculation as to the fate of the dead. He realizes that the new doctrine rests on the faith in a Creator who is bent upon the execution of justice, but with his eyes directed towards life as it presents itself in the world, Koheleth is unwilling to pass beyond actual experience into the realm of nebulous theological speculation, albeit the doctrines derived from such speculations may be reinforced by logical deductions from certain premises. Koheleth is not for that reason atheistically inclined. Far from it. The word God occurs no less than nineteen times in the genuine portions of this little book. He never questions the existence of a supreme Power and the fact that he uses the generic name for deity (Elohim)[78] and never the specific name (Yahweh) of the national deity is a welcome indication that he has passed beyond the stage of any narrow nationalistic conception in his religious attitude. God for him is a Power of universal scope, as in general he has thrown off any particularistic view which would single out one people as standing in a specifically close relation to the Deity. He is a Jew of the broadest type without a trace of sectarianism. Koheleth never speaks of a chosen people, but always of the "children of men," that is, mankind as a whole. As a Sadducee, he would have betrayed his particularism at some point or

[78] See the comment to i. 13 (p. 203).

the other.  He is a theist, because atheism would
have appeared to him to be an illogical assumption of a world coming into existence without
cause and ruled by a blind mechanism.  The God
of Koheleth, however, is not endowed with any
moral attributes.  He represents the Power that is
behind all phenomena, but a Power who, so far as
man is concerned, is beyond knowledge, whose
ways are hidden from mankind and whom man
cannot by searching hope to know.  Koheleth is
consistently averse to speculation either about
nature, life, man or God.  He merely asks us to be
frank enough to look at life as it is.  Everything
lying beyond the evidence of our senses and outside of the realm of experience is unknown and
unknowable.  God, he says (i. 13), has implanted
in us the desire to know things, He has given us
(iii. 11) the capacity to grasp the world with our
intellect, but without the power to carry our
search to any satisfactory conclusion.  Again
and again he impresses upon us the hopelessness
of fathoming the mysteries of existence.[79]  Man cannot know "the work of God who makes all things."[80]
Judging solely by the evidence of our senses, death
appears to be the end of man as of the beast.  The
common experience teaches us that the future
is hidden from us, and that through wisdom
we are not brought nearer to a penetration into
God's work.

[79] Chapter iii. 11; vii. 14; viii. 17; ix. 12.
[80] Chapter xi. 5.

Looking at life as it actually presents itself, there are only two conclusions that can be safely drawn, one that mere ambition is useless, since it brings neither happiness nor illumination, and the other that life is made for enjoyment. Both conclusions are set forth at the close of the decisive test which Koheleth undertook, only to find out that all achievements and all pleasures end in *ennui*. Since, moreover, there is a common fate to all—to the wise and the foolish alike—(ii. 16; ix. 2) the more logical corollary would be to regard life itself as useless. Koheleth actually says so in one place (ii. 17), "I hated life, for all that happened under the sun seemed evil to me, since all was vanity and chasing after wind," but it is the only passage in the book in which this thought is expressed. As a matter of fact, Koheleth loves life, and this inconsistency, of which there are other examples, adds to the charm of the book. "As a living dog," runs a passage that has become famous, "one is better off than a dead lion" (ix. 4). His reason for giving the preference to the dog is, to be sure, not very comforting—nor complimentary to the dog—"for the living" —he adds—"at least know that they will die, whereas the dead know absolutely nothing." His pessimism, however, is only skin deep and, like most pessimists, he clings to life. Job, who is *not* a pessimist, for a moment may think of suicide as a means of putting an end to his sufferings. The suggestion is made to him by his wife,[81] but he rejects it. Koheleth may talk about hating life. He may praise the dead as better off than those who are alive and add "better than both is the one who has not yet been, who has not seen the evil happenings under the sun" (iv. 3), but he does not really think this. Pessimists talk that way, but there are few instances of pessimists deliberately shuffling off the mortal coil against which they rail. They get rid of any suicidal tendencies by writing long disquisitions on the uselessness of life. Schopenhauer, the most eminent of modern pessimists, is a notable example of the care which pessimists take to preserve their health.[82] In reality, the pessimist believes with Koheleth (xi. 7) "Light is sweet and it is pleasant for the eyes to see the sun." The real Koheleth reveals himself in this sentiment, as in the advice to "eat drink, and be merry" which repeated half a dozen times forms[83] the supplement to the constant refrain, "All is vanity and chasing after wind."

To hate all ambition, however, is consistent with the conclusion that finds in enjoyment the solace for life's misery. Accordingly Koheleth emphasizes the reason for "hating" all his toil (ii. 18). Why make work the aim and content of life, since all that you obtain in return for your trouble and vexation is the doubtful privilege of leaving what you have acquired to someone who will enjoy it without having worked for it (ii. 19)?

---

[81] Chapter ii. 9 "Curse God and die"—an euphemism for "do away with thyself."
[82] It is well known that Schopenhauer had a horror of death.
[83] See note 84.

You may be wise, but the chances are that your heir will be a fool; and at all events your days of pain and nights of worry are all to no purpose. Again (iii. 1-2 and 9), since everything that happens is foreordained to occur at the time proper to it, why exert yourself since what is to happen will take place, independently of any efforts on your part. Man labors, Koheleth tells, either from the ambition to outstrip his fellows (iv. 4), or to amass wealth (v. 9). Both motives are "vanity and chasing after wind." What possible satisfaction can there be in rivalry? Surely coöperation is better than competition, for as the commentator to the passage (iv. 9-12) emphasizes, with a partner instead of a rival your business will grow in amount and you will be less liable to collapse in case of business failure. It will be easier to get on your feet again with the help of a partner. In the struggle for life, two against one have a better chance than one against two. As for wealth (v. 10), the more you have, the greater the obligations that are imposed upon you. Your household increases. Others live on your profits, and your only satisfaction is to look at what you have amassed—a melancholy reward for all your toil.

## XIX

### A GENTLE CYNIC

Is it logical to conclude from premises such as these, as Koheleth does, that "There is nothing better for man to do than 'to eat, drink, and to have a good time'"?[84] Hardly. If he were a consistent pessimist, he would urge his readers "to hate life," as he inadvertently does in one passage.[85] His advice would be to escape life, by suicide or by withdrawing from all the idle pleasures of the world. But asceticism is as far removed from Koheleth's frame of mind, as is the Buddhistic doctrine of making life a preparation for complete extinction, without the consciousness that, according to Semitic beliefs, follows man beyond the grave. It is precisely in the corollary "eat, drink, and be merry" to the refrain of "all is vanity," that Koheleth reveals himself as the *gentle* cynic. Do not take life seriously, or at all events not too seriously, is the sum and substance of his philosophy. Even enjoyment must not be taken too seriously. You will tire of it, as Solomon grew weary of all his pleasures, but it is the best thing that you can do under the circumstances. Life has no goal—therefore, smile at life, and pity those who live under the delusion that life is a very serious business. This ironical attitude towards the fleeting panorama of human existence naturally aroused the opposition of the pious and orthodox towards the book. By his illogical conclusion, he aimed a fatal blow at the whole structure of Judaism which rests on the belief in man as God's choicest handiwork—the crowning act of creation, placed here by a just and good Providence.

---

[84] Chapter ii. 24 and repeated with variations iii. 12-13 and 22; v. 17; viii. 15; ix. 7-10; xi. 7-10.
[85] See above p. 136.

"Life is real, life is earnest" was the doctrine that grew up out of the prophet's conception of religion. Koheleth says that life is a shadow, without substance. It cannot be earnest because it has no aim. But why, then, enjoyment as the best way of spending one's days on earth? Simply, because there *is* nothing else to do, certainly nothing better. Koheleth does not preach happiness as the goal of life, but as the only means of not being overwhelmed by the sadness of life, which must ensue if you have the courage to look at things as they are.

Without formulating a system—which would be distasteful to Koheleth's light and easy-going nature—he proceeds to show that his advice is in accord with God's plans for man, so far as we can detect any plan. Unless we try to forget what life really is by enjoying our days, we involve ourselves in a tangle of arguments from which there is no escape. He has already proved[86] that work cannot be the purpose of life, for work ends in leaving the fruits of your labors to those who will care nothing about you. You will be forgotten, while others enjoy. Nor can the purpose of life be to ascertain the meaning of existence, to contemplate the works of God and penetrate to the core of things. God is past finding out. Man cannot know what God is doing (iii. 11). The future is hidden from man as behind a veil, and though a wise man may think that he has solved the riddle

[86] See above, p. 137.

of the universe, it is a delusion pure and simple
(viii. 17). All that man can ascertain as the result
of his search through wisdom and knowledge is
that the happenings of this world are preordained
by God and take place in the order and at the
time determined by the great Power who governs
all things—in nature and in human existence. Is
Koheleth then a fatalist? Surely, but he is as inconsistent in his fatalism as in his pessimism.
The time when a man is to be born is fixed as is the
time of his death (iii. 2)—fixed as definitely as the
time for sowing seeds and for pulling up the ripened plant. If everything is preordained, it is
idle to make the effort to change things. Koheleth's
conclusion from his fatalistic outlook upon life is
to discourage those who believe that the aim of life
is to work for reforms and improvement, to leave
the world better than they found it, even though
it be only a trifle better.

Such an aim is an idle hope—"vanity and
chasing after wind"—as much as is the search for
wisdom and the amassing of wealth. It is a delusion to suppose that one can really *do* anything in
a world entirely controlled by a supreme Spirit—
aye, it is presumptuous to make the attempt. Man
can add nothing to what God does, as little as he
can take anything away (iii. 14). To try "to make
that straight which He (*i.e.*, God) has made
crooked" (vii. 13) is to interfere with God's plans,
to play the part of Providence. You must content
yourself with taking things as they are, and to

remember that prosperity and adversity (or what you consider as such) are both the work of God (vii. 14). As for the meaning of this constant alternation of joy and sorrow, abandon the effort to fathom the mystery. God purposely permits the one to follow the other, so as to prevent you from divining the future. With this thought that God does not want man to solve the problem of life, Koheleth may be said to have reached the extreme point of separation from the orthodox and conventional point of view, not so much, however, in the thought itself as in his manner of putting it. That God's ways are past finding out was good orthodox doctrine, following upon the spiritual conception of a divine Providence who works in a mysterious way, but with the doctrine went the faith that a good and just God *must* do all things for the best. At this point, Koheleth parts company from orthodoxy and boldly asserts that from the evidence furnished by human experience one has no warrant for such faith. If things are pre-ordained, it not only follows that it is presumptuous to look upon one's aim in life to bring about an improvement in the lot of mankind, to correct abuses, to help the needy, to instruct the ignorant, to correct the erring, but it also follows that you must take things as they are and as they come.

Now what do we actually find in the world in which we live and have our being? The cynic, though still a gentle one, steps in and tells us. How is it possible to believe that the world is

governed by a just Power when we encounter—
as we constantly do—wickedness enthroned where
righteousness should be (iii. 16) and oppression
everywhere with no relief in sight (iv. 1)? Koheleth is aware of the stock argument, which is also
brought forward in the Book of Job to justify a
topsy-turvy world, by saying that suffering and
the apparent triumph of wrong is permitted by
God as a test of man's calibre and that in the
end—as the commentator adds (iii. 17)—God will
judge the righteous and the wicked, with the implication that the innocent sufferers will receive
their reward for having endured the test, and that
the wrongdoers will meet their punishment. What
is the value of such a test, asks Koheleth, as a
means of ascertaining who are genuinely virtuous
and God-fearing and who are not? What does
such a test show except that man is as the beast?
Some beasts are happy because they are permitted
to lead a peaceful life, others are hunted down
through no fault of their own. The inequality in
the fortunes of men is of the same order and—what
makes the analogy complete—man and beast die
alike. "All are of the dust and all return to dust."
There is no assurance that man's spirit ascends
after death, and that the spirit of the beast de-
scends (iv. 21). Koheleth's argument is that the
test made by God is to no purpose, since there
is no recompense for suffering and injustice. The
virtuous die under the test, and the wicked thrive
despite the test.

The test, therefore, merely ends in the certainty that man and beast share the same fate. Were Koheleth a genuine pessimist, he might have urged the chilly consolation of the Stoic that one should be resigned to one's fate and suffer in patience, but he is too human not to be deeply stirred by the sufferings of mankind. Briefly but eloquently he describes the sad contrast between "the tears of the oppressed without anyone to console them" and the violence of their oppressors (iv. 1). Tears *versus* Power—such is the world in which men live. So it has always been and so it will continue to be. Are not the dead happier, therefore, because relieved of suffering and of the sight of suffering? Are not those happiest of all who have never been born? We know that Koheleth does not think so, but he puts the question in order to illustrate more forcibly the point that he has in mind, to wit, that there is no satisfactory solution to the problem with which the author of Job grapples—the reason for the triumph of wrong, and for unjust suffering in a world created by a good Power, who stamps His creation with His trade-mark "And God saw that it was good." The problem, it must be borne in mind, arises *only* with the advanced conception of divine government of the universe, which replaces the old view of many gods as personifications of the powers manifesting themselves in nature—the power of the sun, the power of fire, the power of the earth, of the storm or what not—by a single Force, spiritually conceived in terms of ethics. The chief attribute of the old gods is strength, as against justice tempered with mercy and love which are the attributes of the spiritual Being, presiding over the destinies of mankind. As long as Yahweh was merely the national deity of the Hebrews, whose protection and supervision were limited to one particular group, the arbitrariness of his activity was taken for granted. He had his favorites and he could manifest his anger at his pleasure. The task of his worshippers was limited to efforts to secure his protection by bribes in the form of sacrifices, and by flatteries in the form of incantations and direct appeals. But when Yahweh becomes a Being who demands obedience to high ethical standards as a condition of His favor, the corollary is necessarily drawn that God Himself is good and just. Such a Being *cannot* brook injustice, because contrary to the self-imposed laws by means of which He rules the universe. At this stage the vexing problem arises with which religious minds ever since have grappled, how to reconcile the existence of evil and injustice in the world with the conception of a good and just God. The author of the book of Job struggles earnestly and pathetically with this momentous question. The author of Koheleth tackles it lightly and in a semi-ironical spirit. He holds the mirror up to the real world and asks us to look at the image reflected therein.

Both Job and Koheleth, however, represent the reaction on those who had the courage to face the facts of existence against what had come to be the conventional religious view of a world in which—as was assumed—goodness and justice must be triumphant, because the supreme Ruler possesses these attributes. The Book of Job in its original form ends in a *non liquet,* in a practical admission that the problem is insoluble with a faint suggestion, however, as a crumb of comfort, that what may be hidden from us may nevertheless rest on a basis of divine equity. There *may* be a compensation for innocent suffering, but such a possibility is concealed behind a thick mist through which the human mind cannot penetrate. Koheleth says—why try to solve the problem? It will be of no use, for arguments cannot change facts, and the solution, if one could be found, will not mitigate the injustice and suffering in the world. It does not ease Job's pain when suffering the tortures of the damned to be told that it is all a test—even if it were true; and it would only increase his misery to become convinced that he must have committed some misdeed, which is certainly not true, for the point is that Job was "God fearing and removed from evil." By all means, believe in a just and merciful Providence if you can, says Koheleth, but be frank enough to recognize that you "cannot fathom the work of God from the beginning to the end" (iii. 11). Do not delude yourself with high-sounding phrases that are empty of meaning. The jargon of the pious merely serves to close your eyes to the wrongs that are being done, and to shut your ears against hearing the pitiful cries of those who suffer for no good reason. Tears *versus* Power—such is the world.

One thing, however, we do know, namely, that joy makes life bearable; and since everything that happens is ordained of God, happiness should be looked upon as a "gift of God" (iii. 13, v. 18), it comes from "the hand of God" (ii. 24) and is "man's portion" (iii. 22). Joy is approved by God (v. 19); it is a sign that "God approves of man's works" (ix. 7). The variations in the expressive phrase used by Koheleth to justify his conclusion that man should spend his life in joy are not accidental; they are introduced to emphasize in every possible way that the one thing certain among the uncertainties of the world is—happiness.

## XX

### KOHELETH AND GREEK THOUGHT

Is Koheleth to be called a Hedonist—an adherent of the philosophy that looked upon "pleasure" (*hēdonē*) as the aim of life? Is he a follower of Epicurus, because of his oft-repeated advice to "eat, drink, and be merry," which he carries so far as to urge the young to "follow the inclinations of their minds and the sight of their eyes" (xi. 9)? Some scholars have seen in this aspect of Koheleth's attitude toward life the reflex of Greek philosophy, as they also attribute his skepticism in regard to a just Providence to the spread of Greek philosophy among the Jews. No doubt Greek thought, as a significant phase of Greek culture, must have made its influence felt in Palestine where Koheleth lived, with the influx of Greek ideas, with the adoption of Greek forms of government and the imitation of Greek modes of life throughout the Orient after the conquests of Alexander the Great (334-323 B.C.). The Greek spirit, we have seen, tended towards individualism;[87] it promoted independent thought, leading on the one hand to the definite recognition of authorship in literary production, and on the other to the rise of systems of philosophy, associated with individual thinkers—Pythagoras, Heraclitus, Democritus, Epicurus, Zeno, Socrates, Plato, and Aristotle. The chief outcome, however, of Greek culture in the intellectual domain was, outside of art, the giving rise to the *scientific* spirit, substituting astronomy for astrology without, to be sure, suppressing the latter entirely, giving to medicine, up to that time a purely empirical art, a more scientific aspect by the study of anatomy and physiology, and promoting the exact study of the forces of nature and the structure of animals. Koheleth betrays to a considerable extent the influence of this scientific spirit. His observations on nature, especially in the introduction to the book, lead him to recognize the invariability of the laws of the universe. He knows that dreams come from too much business (v. 2.), that is, from mental activity continued during sleep. The interpreta-

[87] See above, p. 39.

tion of dreams is, therefore, an idle pursuit. Perhaps the experience that overeating is not conducive to sleep (v. 11) may have been gained without any knowledge of the reason therefor, but certainly the manner of stating that the hard worker sleeps "whether he has eaten little or much" sounds as though the author had evolved a theory of the cause of sleep. Significant is the knowledge of the structure of the body and the function of the human organs revealed in the impressive closing chapter of the book.[88] There is a system in the successive enumeration of the hips, legs, teeth, eyes, ears, voice and hair, as in the recognition of the function of the brain, spine, and kidneys, though veiled under poetic metaphors. On the basis of this chapter Professor Haupt concludes that Koheleth must have been a physician,[89] which may well have been the case. Certainly he must have known something of the theories and experiments of the Greek schools of medicine, following along the path marked out by Hippocrates. We also know from the discussions of the Rabbis in the Talmud that the Greek systems of philosophy had made their way into Palestine and Babylonia during the last two centuries preceding our era, while in Alexandria we note the rise of a system of philosophy in the century before this era, which attempts to reconcile the speculations and conclusions of Greek philoso-

---

[88] See the comments to this chapter, p. 238 *et seq.*
[89] "The Book of Ecclesiastes" in "Oriental Studies" (Philadelphia, 1894) p. 238 *et seq.*, p. 275 (note 60).

phers with Jewish theology, and of which we find significant traces in the Gospel of John and in the Pauline epistles.[90]

The spirit of Greek philosophy was at all times hostile to the prevailing beliefs among the Greeks. Plato alone appears to have made an attempt to save some fragments out of the wreck of Greek mythology, through the rise of systems which found no place for the gods of ancient Greece. The tone of Koheleth when he deals with the naïve conception of divine government that marked the pious adherents of Judaism is not unlike the somewhat patronizing attitude of Greek philosophers towards the conventional religion, which they hardly regarded as of sufficient moment to warrant an energetic campaign against it. The old structure, they felt, was shaken in its foundations and was destined to give way without any direct attack. Koheleth is too good-natured to oppose the theology that arose from the new conception of religion brought forward by the prophets. He tolerates it, but he shows by insinuation rather than by any polemical disposition how insufficient it is as a means of explaining the actual conditions of life. His skepticism is of an easy-going character, as his cynicism is always gentle, with only an occasional sting. In his general attitude towards the Judaism of his day, which on the ceremonial side—sacrifices and inquiries of priests

[90] See Schuerer, "The History of the Jewish People in the time of Jesus Christ," ii. 3, p. 381, or Edward Caird, "Evolution of Theology in the Greek Philosophers, ii., p. 357 *et seq*.

as to the significance of dreams and portents—
was full of survivals of primitive points of view,
we may recognize the influence of the new spirit
that had come into the land with the advent of
the Greeks. But we must not press this influence too hard, and attempt to see in Koheleth's
view of predestination and of submission to fate
the teachings of the Greek Stoics, or make him an
adherent of the school of Heraclitus or Epicurus,
because of his advocacy of enjoyment as the legitimate function of existence. He is not the type
of mind that follows strictly and consistently any
particular school of thought. He goes his own way
in setting before us the picture of the world, as it is
reflected in his mind. Above all, he would lay no
claim to being consistent. We have seen that he
does not draw the conclusion, from his view of all
things being predetermined by God, that man lacks
freedom of will. It is doubtful whether he would
quite have understood the meaning of the technical term; and he merely goes so far as to discourage the effort of man to improve things, as
though this were the aim of life. That is not
man's business. If there is to be any improvement
—and Koheleth sees no evidence for this, but
merely endless repetition—it must be left to God.
Do what lies immediately before you and do it
to the full, "for there is no activity, no reckoning,
no knowledge and no wisdom in Sheol whither
thou goest" (ix. 10). As for the rest, enjoy yourself as much as you can.

It is sufficient, therefore, to assume that contact with Greek culture lent a stimulus to independent thought among the Jews; it helped to accentuate the difficulties involved in accepting the implications of a faith that placed at the head of the universe a Power for good, but who permitted evil to flourish in a world of His making. The problem itself, however, was a Jewish one, insofar as it represented the reaction against the conventional piety which grew up on the basis of the distinctively ethical monotheism of the Jews. It is not necessary to pass outside of a Jewish environment in order to explain either the trend of Koheleth's thought or his conclusions, beyond the initial impulse towards independent thought which through the spread of Greek culture in the Orient had become part of the spirit of the age. Koheleth was caught by the *Zeitgeist*, but without becoming an adherent of any particular school—Greek or otherwise.

## XXI

### KOHELETH'S ATTITUDE TOWARDS THE CULT

The further justification in thus regarding Koheleth as a free lance, following the drift of his own thought into whatever direction his changing fancy, his good humor, and his human sympathies —under a mask of gentle irony—led him, is to be found in his easy-going and not altogether consistent attitude towards religious worship, towards affairs of government, towards women, and above all in his view that although enjoyment of life is the best way of spending one's days, yet even of this one will tire, and finally that toil is to be joined to sipping the honey out of the flower of existence.

To go to the temple for the purpose of offering sacrifices is from Koheleth's rationalistic point of view a waste of time (iv. 17), as it is foolish to go to the priest in order to receive an interpretation of a dream or to obtain an oracle of any kind. "God is in heaven and thou art upon earth. Therefore, let thy words be few" (v. 1). There is no use in reciting long formulas, for God will nevertheless bring to pass what is going to happen. The priests cannot help you, and appeals to God are not going to change His plans. That is bold language, and for once Koheleth even passes beyond the bounds of what we would call courteous discussion by his insinuation that the priest is a fool (iv. 17); or if it is not the priest to whom the epithet is applied, then it is the one who brings the sacrifice.

To be sure, Koheleth makes an attempt to take off the keen edge of his sharp attack on the senselessness of worship by suggesting that one should "go to the house of God to hear" (iv. 17). One is tempted to conclude from this that, at the time that Koheleth wrote, a discourse formed part of the temple service. The synagogue as the laymen's temple had already made its appearance in the second century before our era.[91] It began as an "assembly"—such is the meaning of *sunagōgē*—

---

[91] See Schuerer, "The History of the Jewish People in the Time of Jesus Christ," ii. 2, p. 54 *et seq.*

of laymen for the study of the Law. Around this study a religious service grew up and on certain days, notably on the Sabbath, a portion of the Law was expounded for the benefit of the public. This practice in turn became the starting-point of the sermon as a feature both of the Jewish and of the Christian Church. Whether in the official center of worship at Jerusalem where priests officiated and sacrifices were brought, the custom of expounding the law had also been introduced is not certain, but it is not improbable that the example of the synagogue was imitated in the "central" sanctuary as an innovation, calculated to increase the attachment of the worshippers to the official cult. The Law at all events was read, and Koheleth puts his stamp of approval on this part of the service. To listen to sound advice, he says, can do you only good. The temple officials, however, could hardly have been satisfied with such a concession, for to them as to the orthodox adherents of the Judaism of the day the traditional sacrifices, as perscribed by the Law, constituted the essential feature of the public cult.

Koheleth, again, offended the priests and the laity alike by his evident contempt for those who rushed to the temple to make vows which in many cases, he insinuates, were prompted by a sudden emotion only to be forgotten when the cause for the emotion had passed by. A man in business distress or in trouble of some other kind or when

seized with illness might make a vow to do certain
things in case of relief, and in human fashion would
forget all about it when things again went well.
Koheleth's irony passes over into biting sarcasm
when he suggests that the one who is reminded of
the vow will pretend that it was a slip—was not
seriously meant (v. 5). Why arouse the anger of
God through urging lame excuses, when the fact
is that you merely made a vow in the hope of thus
escaping from a dangerous crisis? Koheleth has no
patience with any form of hypocrisy or self-
deception. It is clear that he is hitting hard at
certain evils in religion which must have been
quite common, but the situation that he depicts
is evidently one that grew out of the decline of the
hold which the temple and its cult once had upon
the people. The pious members of the community
had begun to turn to the synagogues, which became
centers of serious religious study and were destined
to be the bulwarks of Judaism when the temple
service finally came to an end upon the destruction
of the sanctuary in 70 A.D.

The references in the Talmud and in Josephus
to the quarrels among the priesthood and to the
growing degeneracy of the official cult confirm the
unfavorable picture that we obtain from the New
Testament of conditions in the temple at Jerusalem in the days of Jesus. The temple ritual rested
on a foundation, incompatible with the worship of
a spiritually conceived God of the universe. The
force of tradition and the practical impossibility

of a religious organization to cut loose from old associations combined to reintroduce a cult which the pre-exilic prophets had denounced as leading to the very evils which again flourished in Koheleth's days, though not to the same extent as in the days of the monarchy, when the temple was purely the adjunct of the state. The synagogue as an institution is an outcome of post-exilic Judaism; the temple is a survival of the old Yahwism carried over into the new era. Koheleth would approve of the synagogue as a center for religious study, but he can see no purpose in an institution like the temple, with rites that were incompatible with the advanced religious ideas which had spread among the people, through the influence of the prophets. For all that, it must have been distasteful, even to those who recognized the justice of Koheleth's indictment of the stupidity or hypocrisy of the priests and the absurdity of the temple rites, to have the truth so bluntly put.

## XXII

### KOHELETH ON "REFORM," ROYALTY, AND WOMAN

Even more distasteful to the powers that be must have been Koheleth's exposure of the corruption that, according to him, inevitably eats its way into government, and of the arbitrariness and haughtiness that appear to be the prerogatives of royalty. Bad as is the oppression of the poor and the perversion of justice, what is still worse is the impossibilility of getting at those who are really responsible for the distressing conditions in the state. Koheleth has no confidence in reform movements, arising through indignation at the discovery of corruption, but which fail to remove the cause. Do not be amazed, he says, at finding out how rotten things are, for there is always some one "higher up" who is responsible and whom you cannot reach (v. 7). In guarded language, the text of which may have been interfered with in order to remove the suspicion of *lèse-majesté*, he suggests that if we were to follow this attempt to get the one "higher up," the quest would end with the one at the "top"—that is, with the king.

In keeping with this gloomy picture of the hopelessness of bringing about improvements in government and in social conditions that follow upon a government honey-combed with corruption, Koheleth ironically advises one not to rush into the royal presence for the purpose of making complaint (viii. 3). You will get no sympathy. The king will do whatever he pleases, and all that you will get for your pains is a dismissal from the office that you may hold. It is the part of discretion to obey the king's command. Who can say to a king, "What art thou doing?" (viii. 4.) Discretion is the better part of valor. If the king is angry, try to pacify him. Do not resign your position, for that will only be looked upon as an acknowledgment of guilt (x. 4). Be careful in what you say and do. Koheleth ironically suggests that even your thoughts in the solitude of your bed-chamber may get you into trouble. The walls have ears.

*modern*

> "Do not, even on thy couch, defame a king,
> Nor in thy bed-chamber denounce a rich man,
> For a bird of heaven will carry the sound,
> And a winged creature will reveal the utterance." (x. 20.)

Not an agreeable picture, forsooth, of espionage in ancient Palestine!

Kingship rested throughout antiquity on the basis of divine right.[92] The king owed his position to the belief that he was supposed to be the representative of the national deity on earth—his terrestrial vicar. He was the visible lieutenant of the invisible general. Hence the logical theory of the descent of kings from the gods so common in antiquity and of which we have some survivals in our days. William II. still believed in it, with consequences disastrous to his people and to himself. The king is the earliest type of "the son of God." Among the Egyptians and Assyrians the kings are actually designated as the sons of some god or the other. He is "named" by the god to occupy the throne; and the idea of direct sonship shades over almost imperceptibly into the doctrine of the incarnation of the God in an earthly representative. The glamor of royalty arises from this view of the position of the king. Koheleth, realizing the absurdity of a theory which would invest an ordinary human being with superhuman prerogatives, brushes it away by a single sweep.

[92] See Sir Jas. G. Frazer, "Early History of Kingship," p. 32, *et seq.*

A poor and wise child is superior to a king who is old and foolish (iv. 13). How can one believe in a hereditary kingdom of divine origin, when one sees that through a rebellion or conspiracy a king may be driven from his throne, and a person poor and of humble birth may pass on to the royal throne (iv. 14). But the glory of the new king is also destined to pass away. Be he received with ever so great an enthusiasm by virtue of his youth and of his success, he too will grow old and the hopes centered in him will fade away. The rejoicing at the change will cease, when it is recognized that things follow in the same groove. "Surely this is vanity and chasing after wind" (iv. 15-16). Royal splendor is as fleeting as everything else in this world. Moreover, what is this vaunted power of the king? Koheleth has just told us that the king does what he pleases, but even the king has no power over the wind or over death; and if God has so decreed, he as little as anyone else can escape his fate in war (viii. 8).

Koheleth's reflections on the corruption of government and on the arbitrariness of rulers clearly mirror conditions which he saw about him. It is not necessary, therefore, to assume outside influences to account for this attitude towards government, any more than for his views on the futility of the temple cult. He is an observer of human affairs and draws his conclusions from what he has experienced. He is not a closet philosopher who immerses himself in the study of systems of philosophy in order to evolve a system of his own.

Similarly, when he enlarges upon the strange distortions in the world, to further illustrate the vanity of things, he again draws upon his experience and does not speak as the adherent of any particular system of the philosophy of life. He has seen the wicked triumphant in this world, and their glory extending even beyond the grave. They are accorded the distinction of large funerals. The people coming back from the cemetery praise them in the very city in which the wicked dead carried on the mischief that they wrought (viii. 10). As an instance of the ingratitude of the world, he tells the story of a wise man but poor who by his wisdom saved a city from being taken by a powerful king who had besieged it. What happened to the wise man? His great achievement for which no doubt he was commended at the time was forgotten (ix.14-15). The incident clearly rests upon an actual occurrence; and it is characteristic of Koheleth's point of view that he concludes from the occurrence that, despite the neglect to which the wise man was exposed, wisdom is better than mere strength (ix. 16). This is another proof that Koheleth's pessimism is only skin deep or he would have asked, What is the use of being wise? His pessimism neither affects his humor nor his sound sense. All that he asks of us is to have the courage to face the facts. Do not expect too much of the world, but do not for that reason give yourself up to despair. Above all do not imagine as you grow old that things were better in former days. Koheleth has no use for the *laudatores temporis acti,* who are constantly decrying the present and idealizing the past. The man who suggests that "the former days were better than these" (vii. 10) is not betraying superior wisdom. He is merely suffering from mental arteriosclerosis. The processes of his mind have grown sluggish with age, as the blood courses less freely through the veins, and he is unable to keep pace with the more rapidly moving age. Koheleth hits hard at the conservatism of advancing years, which he thus mercilessly analyzes as not due to increasing wisdom but to increasing age, heralding the approach of the time when, as he says in the last chapter, one loses the zest for life, "the evil days of which thou shalt say, I have no pleasure in them" (xii. 1).

Nor need we assume outside influence to account finally for Koheleth's mistrust of women. The pleasures of youth and manhood are largely taken up with sensual delights in which feminine charms naturally play a large part. As a frank observer, Koheleth declines to take a prudish view of the "eternal feminine" that lures us on. But as all pleasures pall in time, so a time comes when the attractions of woman no longer arouse the senses, and when this moment comes one discovers that of all things that are vain and empty woman takes the lead. The main attraction of woman according to Koheleth lies in her charm,

not in her character. When that charm goes or
when we are no longer sensitive to it, the illu-
sion is "more bitter than death." (vii. 26.)
"Her mind is all snares and nets, her hands are
fetters" is merely the Oriental way of phrasing
"the lure of the feminine," with a touch of bitterness that suggests an outburst due to personal
experience. Renan[93] was probably not the first to
suspect that Koheleth was a bachelor, but the very
vehemence of his indictment that he has failed to
find a decent woman among a thousand (vii. 28)
points to his having been not altogether insensible
to female charms. The large number need not be
taken literally, and one feels that Koheleth is bent
upon having his little joke—now grown somewhat
stale by incessant repetition for over two thousand years—at the expense of woman. Koheleth
could be certain also of finding an appreciative
audience for his joke, for in the ancient as in the
modern Orient woman plays a prominent part in
the life of man, though more as his tool than as
his partner.

The Book of Proverbs reveals woman much
in the same light as she appears in Koheleth. We
have, to be sure, the eloquent and beautiful praise
of the virtuous housewife in the last chapter of
Proverbs, but one suspects that this late appendix[94]

---

[93] Introduction to "L'Ecclésiaste," p. 89.

[94] Prov. xxxi. 10-31 without any connection with what precedes and
not in the crisp epigrammatic style of the bulk of the collection. The first
letters of the 22 verses follow the order of the Hebrew alphabet--another
indication of its late date and of its rather artificial composition.

was added by some pious writer to present a counter-picture to the portrayal of the charmer and ensnarer in chapters v, vi, vii, and elsewhere.[95]

> "Can a man take fire in his bosom and his clothes
>     not be burned,
> Or can he walk upon hot coals and his feet not be
>     scorched?"  (vi. 27–28.)

Though the metaphor is applied to the bad woman yet the prominence given in Proverbs to the warnings against her is an indication of the general attitude towards woman as the tempter. The view is in accord with the picture drawn of the first woman in the third chapter of Genesis, and which finds an echo in the sayings of Ben Sira (xxv. 24).

> "From a woman was the beginning of sin, and
>     because of her we all die."

*Cherchez la femme*, we must bear in mind, is ortho- dox Biblical doctrine, and it was no small matter to trace to the female allurement the hard lot of man on earth to work for his food instead of find- ing it hanging on trees in a park. The wives of the patriarchs are portrayed with serious blemishes. Sarah lies and is severely rebuked by her husband.[96] She is also envious and heartless.[97] Rebecca de- deceives her husband[98] and Rachel is jealous.[99] In the historical annals women are rarely held up

---

[95] Prov. xxiii. 26-28. Three times the saying is repeated (xxi. 9 and 19; xxv. 24) that living in a garret (or on a desert island) is better than life with a contentious woman. See also Proverbs xxvii. 15–16 and xxx. 23.

[96] Genesis xviii. 15.

[97] Witness her treatment of Hagar and Ishmael (Gen. xvi. 6 and xxi. 8 *et seq.* [98] Genesis xxvii. 6-17. [99] Genesis xxx. 1.

as models. David and Solomon are led astray by women, and the queens of the two kingdoms are greater sinners than the kings. The bad woman must have become a common figure to be introduced by the prophets so frequently as the metaphor to illustrate Israel's falling away from loyalty to Yahweh. Koheleth, therefore, reflects a common Oriental view in not having a very exalted opinion of woman. Had he come strongly under Greek influence, instead of merely receiving a stimulus to independent thought from contact with Greek culture, he might have given us a different picture, for Greek literature on the whole, with some notable exceptions, portrays woman as heroic, faithful, self-sacrificing and as an ennobling influence. Helen and Klytemnestra are the exceptions; Hecuba and the heroic women of Troy are the rule.

## XXIII
### "WORK AND PLAY"

But if any further evidence were needed for the thesis here maintained that to account for Koheleth's attitude towards life, including his advice to seek as much enjoyment as possible, we need not look for influences of Greek thought, it would be found in the rather inconsistent combination of toil *with* enjoyment as the best course to follow in life, though both are vain and neither constitutes a real aim. That is not the Greek way of looking at things. The Greek thinker is logical. He starts from some fundamental principle and develops it to a consistent conclusion from the consequences of which he does not shrink. Koheleth is sporadic, and, as illustrated by his book, jumps from one topic to the other, without fear of repeating himself, as he frequently does, or of contradicting himself, of which he is occasionally guilty. He smiles at life and does not want us to take anything too seriously, including himself. He is not a theorist and, therefore, he realizes that although enjoyment alone makes life tolerable, activity of some kind is needed in order to keep the appetite for enjoyment whetted. Without toil, one would tire of enjoyment more quickly. His advice "to eat, drink, and be merry" has, therefore, no close affiliation with the doctrine of Epicurus, whose hedonism, besides being a logical outcome of his thought, is of a much more sober character, any more than Koheleth's view of things being preordained by God leads him to more than a superficial approach to the doctrines of Stoicism.

Koheleth looks upon enjoyment as the fruit of labor (iii. 22). He regards it as a misfortune to amass wealth and to acquire fame without the capacity to enjoy. Long life and a large family are blessings of God, according to the Oriental point of view, but they are empty forms without enjoyment. The man who has not enjoyed his life had better not have been born (vi. 3-5). The untimely birth is better off since it has not seen life and, therefore, has not missed the chance for enjoyment. To lose this chance is the greatest of all evils. One loses this chance in various ways, by being too ambitious for worldly success, by being too anxious to heap up silver, but also, as we shall see, by being over-conscientious. Ambition, Koheleth has already told us,[100] is merely the endeavor to outstrip one's neighbor. That is foolish. Work so that you may enjoy your leisure— is the sum and substance of Koheleth's philosophy. Success beyond this is a will-o'-the-wisp. It eludes you—even at the moment when you have grasped it. For look again at things as they are. "The race is not to the swift, nor the battle to the strong" (ix. 11). There is perhaps an autobiographical touch when he adds that "wise men lack an income and prophets do not possess riches." Had Koheleth enjoyed a competency, he would probably have fallen a victim to a more sunny philosophy, for one feels throughout his book that he loved life for the pleasures that it brought.

His pessimism, however, did not penetrate into his soul and embitter it. Hence, he could say with gentle irony and without any bitterness that "time and chance" are the accidental factors that condition what men call worldly success (ix. 11). Besides, what an empty bubble mere success is! In a twinkling, man is caught in the trap set by death, as fish in a net and as birds in a snare (ix. 12). As for amassing wealth, the curse lies in the desire for more, no matter how much one has. "He who loves silver, will never have enough

---

[100] See above, p. 138, 4.

silver" (v. 9). The rich man merely increases his troubles. Having more, simply means that your household expenses increase (v. 10). Koheleth, just because he was not rich, could recognize that the rich are not happier, and that the enjoyment of the millionaire is not infrequently limited to looking at his wealth (v. 10), which some day others who do not care for him will enjoy.

For all that, he counsels work—only not as the *aim* of life but as the *means* of enjoyment. If we are justified in assuming that a portion of the first part of the eleventh chapter[101] formed part of the original book, Koheleth even offers some shrewd business advice to those engaged in mercantile pursuits. He urges them to take some risks, for that is what is meant by the famous phrase (xi. 1)

> "Cast thy bread upon the face of the waters,
>   for after many days thou shalt find it."

The conventional interpretation, as though Koheleth were inculcating charity with an assurance that one will get one's reward, is merely another illustration of the manner in which the entire spirit of the book was altered by the attempt to direct its thought into an orthodox channel. Koheleth is thinking of business ventures in sending out one's goods on ships, and in world-wise fashion he adds the caution not to trust all of your goods in one ship.

> "Divide it up into seven or eight portions,
>   for thou knowest not what will happen on earth" (xi. 2).

[101] Namely, verses 1, 2, 5 and 6 as indicated in the translation.

Do not put all of your investments into one stock, he would tell us to-day, but divide them up into seven or eight companies. Moreover, do not try to forecast all possibilities, but work steadily. No one can tell what part of his activity will be successful, any more than one can forecast the direction of the wind. God alone knows. Therefore,

> "In the morning sow thy seed
> And till evening let not thy hand rest,
> For thou knowest not which will succeed, this or that,
> Or whether both alike shall be good" (xi. 6).

But through thy toil bear in mind that life is pleasant only if it is enjoyed,

> "Though a man live many years, let him be happy throughout"
> (xi. 8).

The happy life is the only life worth living. Only one who loves life could utter such a sentiment, only one who did not allow his humor to be spoiled by taking things too seriously could say as Koheleth does even when life approaches the end,

> "Light is sweet, and it is pleasant for the eyes to see the sun"
> (xi. 7).

Lastly, it is part of Koheleth's philosophy, based on observation of things as they are in this world, to utter a warning against the possible sacrifice of one's chance of enjoyment by going to an extreme in being overconscientious. He is a preacher of sanity and moderation. Things are not as they should be in this world. The wicked, we have seen,[102] sit in the seat of the righteous.

[102] See above, p. 143.

The righteous often incur the fate that should meet the wicked (viii. 14). The bad man is honored even beyond the grave (viii. 10), but for all that if if one sets out, on the basis of this observation, to outdo others in wickedness in the hope of getting the largest return, one will be disappointed. If a man is *too* wicked, he will be found out and meet his just punishment. Don't overdo it, for the world is not quite so bad as, judging from topsy-turvy conditions, it may appear to be. The man who is overwicked overshoots the mark. He is a fool who will die before his time (vii. 17).

But what is the man to do who wishes to be righteous and yet sees the "righteous perishing by his righteousness"? (vii. 15.) Our gentle cynic whispers, "Be not overrighteous nor overwise, why ruin thyself?" (vii. 16.) The cynicism is undisguised, but it is without any sting. Koheleth does not say, "follow the wicked path, provided you do not go at too rapid a pace," but rather utters the warning that, "if you are too wicked, you will get into trouble." At the same time, with a gentle ironical smile playing on his lips, he restrains the idealist from acting as though he were living in a world in which his ideals have been realized. Do not forget that things are most imperfect in this world. Do not walk with your head in the clouds. You will come to grief if you do. Watch your step! You must accommodate yourself to existing circumstances,

" 'Be bold! be bold!' and everywhere, 'Be bold';
  'Be not too bold!' "

reads the wise saying of old.[103] Koheleth might even say of righteousness as Longfellow does of courage: "Yet better the excess than the defect"; but he would add, "Do not allow your conscience, however, to carry you too far above the standards of the world in which you live." The advice is bad —let us not close our eyes to that—but it is not offered in a spirit of bitterness. It comes from one who loves life, despite its drawbacks and its disappointments, and who would spare youth the misery that comes from striking one's head against the stars, with the result of tumbling into a muddy abyss. Do not lose your chance of enjoyment of life by taking yourself too seriously. That is the extent of his gentle cynicism. What will you get for your pains in trying to reform the world, beyond Hamlet's bitter self-reproach,

"The time is out of joint: O cursed spite,
That ever I was born to set it right!"

"Who is able to straighten out what God has made crooked?" (vii. 13.) Take good and evil as they come. Take neither too seriously. Koheleth frankly does not approve of martyrs. They miss enjoyment, and what is life worth without it? Toil is empty without pleasure as its reward, just as pleasure without toil leads to *ennui*. Wisdom, riches, honors, enterprises, royalty, riotous living, woman, aye even piety—all turn out to be vain and afford no permanent satisfaction. Pleasures, too, one tires of, but enjoyment *with* toil at least makes

---

[103] Longfellow's "Morituri Salutamus."

life bearable. One may grow weary even of this combination and eventually find life itself "vanity and chasing after wind," but not at all events before old age comes on, presaging the gradual loss of faculties and the weakening of functions, till at last the inevitable end comes—the common fate to all—"to the righteous and to the wicked, to the good [and bad], to the clean and to the unclean, to the one who sacrifices and to the one who does not sacrifice; as the virtuous so the sinner, the one who swears an oath and the one who fears an oath" (ix. 2). This is the worst of all evils "that there should be one fate to all" (ix. 3). but you will go down to Sheol in a more resigned frame of mind, if you have tasted enjoyment throughout your life.

## XXIV
### JOY THAT IS SANE

Koheleth must be recognized as a cynic but, it is now plain, as a gentle one; he shows himself in this light by preaching moderation, even while urging the young to rejoice in their youth, to be of cheerful mind and to follow their inclinations and the sight of their eyes (xi. 9). Enjoy yourselves! But Koheleth's advice to "eat, drink, and be merry" does not mean riotous living. It does not mean playing the role of the idler and spendthrift, who indulges his passions and seeks for mere physical sensations to stimulate his jaded body. Koheleth's enjoyment of life is that which comes as a respite from toil. Enjoyment without toil is worse than toil

without enjoyment. We may gather this from the
way in which he denounces those who feast in the
morning (x. 16). That is a sign of gluttony—a waste
of time that should be devoted to toil. If he were living to-day, he would rail at those who play bridge in
the morning. One should feast and play at the proper time. Enjoyment should be for recreation "for
strength and not for guzzling" (x. 17). His picture
of a land badly ruled is one governed by a mere
puppet with "princes feasting in the morning,"
in contrast to a country governed by a real king
"with princes feasting at the proper time." Koheleth tells us in more specific terms what kind of
enjoyment he has in mind,

> "Go, eat thy bread with joy,
> And drink thy wine with a merry heart,
> For God has already given His approval to thy deeds.
> At all times be thy garments white,
> And let oil not be lacking for thy head,
> Enjoy life with the woman of thy love. "(ix. 7-9.)

The passage is particularly interesting because of a
remarkable parallel to it that has been found in
Babylonian literature, with so close a resemblance,
indeed, as to raise the question whether Koheleth
may not be quoting from some earlier work, which
may in turn have reverted to a Babylonian pro-
totype. The parallel occurs in the story of the
adventures of a hero who was known as Gish[104]
or Gilgamesh. This epic—for such it is—forms the
most important literary production of ancient Babylonia. With constant additions, it passed down the

[104] Gish means "hero."

ages to Assyria, and we find echoes of this epic in the Greek tale of Hercules and in the legends that gathered around Alexander. Of the entire story, which in its final form was told on twelve tablets of some 250 lines each, not much more than one-half has up to the present been recovered.[105] The particular tablet in which the parallel to the passage in Koheleth occurs dates from about 2000 B.C. and is therefore about 1800 years earlier than Koheleth! Gilgamesh has been smitten with disease as a punishment for having rejected the offer of the goddess Ishtar to become her spouse. This episode of the epic embodies a nature myth. Gilgamesh is in part a human figure, but in part also a god, and more specifically a personification of the sun-god, while Ishtar is the goddess of the earth. The ripening of the fruits of the soil was pictured as the result of a union between the sun and the earth. The sun's rays penetrate the earth, which is the womb of the goddess, and fructify her, but after some months the sun recedes from the earth, and the rains with the accompanying desolation of nature set in. The sun-god after a short union has rejected the advances of the earth. This change of seasons was pictured as an insult offered to Ishtar by Gilgamesh, who now enters upon a long series of wanderings in search for healing from his disease. The sickness of Gilgamesh is the waning of the power of the sun's

---

[105] See my analysis and translation of the Gilgamesh Epic in "The Sacred Books and Early Literature of the East," volume i. pp. 187-220.

rays with the approach of the wintry season.  The
wanderings of the hero represent the course of the
sun through the heavens during the winter months,
seeking for the renewal of his strength which finally
comes with the spring.  In the tale Gilgamesh is
portrayed as coming to a maiden Sabitu, dwelling
at the seashore.  He inquires of her how he can
secure life which he feels to be ebbing away.  To
the "human" Gilgamesh—who alternates in the
story with Gilgamesh the sun-god—the maiden
replies as follows:

"Why, O Gish, dost thou wander about?
The life that thou seekest, thou wilt not find.
When the gods created men,
Death they ordained for men,
Life they kept in their hands.
Thou, O Gish, fill thy belly!
Day and night be joyful!
Daily be glad!
Day and night make merry!
Let thy garments be white,
Annoint thy head, and purify thyself!
With the children at thy side,
Enjoy the wife of thy bosom!"

The parallel is not limited to the similarity of the
advice and to an agreement in the language in
which it is offered, but extends to the spirit that
dictates it.  As in Koheleth there is a note of resignation to be content with life in this world, for
there is nothing to be hoped for in *Aralû*, as the
Babylonians called the great gathering place of the
dead in the subterranean hollow which for
the Hebrews was Sheol.  The dead are conscious

but they have no joy in the nether world. Without joy of what use is consciousness? Therefore, since death is the inevitable fate decreed by the gods, get as much enjoyment out of life as you can while it lasts. Feasting, white garments—white being the color of joy—care and adornment of one's body, happiness with one's wife and children—such is the picture drawn by a Babylonian writer, who lived almost two thousand years before Koheleth. The latter's point of view, therefore, is one that could grow up in a Semitic environment at any time, without outside influence. The undercurrent of resignation to the inevitable also shows itself in Koheleth. Sleep after toil is sweet.

> "Sweet is the sleep of the laborer, whether he has eaten
> little or much" (v. 11)

but ever the shadow of the coming end is thrown across man's pathway. This tempers one's joy and creates the mood which prompts Koheleth to denounce the emptiness of life.

> "The day of death is better than the day of birth.
> It is better to go to the house of mourning than to a
> house of feasting,
> For the former marks the end of all men." (vii. 2.)

The pious commentator who adds "And the living will take it to mind," has missed the point, as has the one who adds, "Dissatisfaction is better than laughter." Koheleth would reject the latter sentiment completely, nor does he believe in sorrow as a mental discipline, as the pious commentator suggests (vii. 3<sup>b</sup>). The "house of feasting" is the author's phrase for riotous living, for shallow pleasures as the sole aim of one's life. To recognize the seriousness of life, aye, its sad aspects through the injustice and corruption that prevail in the world, is part of Koheleth's gospel, and indeed is as essential to his thought as is the aim to get enjoyment out of it. One should be mindful even in one's joy of what life means to those who have sorrow and who are bound down by its worries. He does not advise going about with a long face, but neither does he approve of those who act as though life were all fun. The empty chatter that one hears in a house given up to mirth is not the kind of joy that Koheleth has in mind, and therefore he can consistently with his gospel of joy declare,

"The mind of the wise is in a house of mourning,
but the mind of fools is in the house of mirth." (vii. 4.)

You can hear some sound talk in a house into which death has entered. A funeral sermon, Koheleth might have added, had he lived in more modern times, is apt to be better than an after-dinner speech, which he would often have found to be "full of sound and fury—signifying nothing."

That life is made for enjoyment, sums up Koheleth's philosophy, but the reverse proposition that enjoyment is the *aim* of life is not true. To make enjoyment the aim leads to excesses, to "feasting in the morning," to making life consist of idle chatter and foolish laughter, to complete exhaustion of one's senses and—to *ennui*.

The most discouraging feature of Koheleth's attitude towards life is the constant undercurrent of the "one fate to all," of the "place to which all must go," of the end that overtakes the wise as the fool, the righteous and the wicked. Nevertheless, if he were a real pessimist down to the bone he would have struck a different key throughout the book. Even though he might have felt that he was deceiving himself he would have assumed an attitude of disgust with life, and suggested that death was to be regarded as a release from the entanglements and disappointments of a cruel and wicked world. To be sure, he says that "the end is better than the beginning" (vii. 8), but we know from the whole tenor of his thought that he does not believe it. He is too honest not to let us see even when he rails against the various kinds of vanity in the world, that "light is sweet" to him, that he loves life as such. Though he has grown old—for only an old man could have given the beautiful and impressive picture of old age at the end of the book —he still clings to life, if only because of the recollections of the joys which he has tasted. He must have had his trials and disappointments. He is disillusioned in regard to the *value* of life, he realizes that things cannot be improved, but he is also sensible enough to see that the past was no better than the present (vii. 10). He knows from experience that wisdom cannot help us to discern the aim of existence nor to penetrate the mystery of the future. He sees men struggling for wealth and fame, setting aside ideals in the struggle—and he smiles at all this vanity. He knows that there is much injustice and innocent suffering—and again he smiles at those who take such conditions too seriously. His cynicism is gentle—resolving itself into the formula, "Work and Play." Enjoy life while it lasts, for it is pleasant to see the sun, despite everything that "happens under the sun." Koheleth would have espoused the sentiment with which Renan—a modern Koheleth—closes his delightful *Souvenirs d'enfance et de jeunesse* in thanking the author of his being for the "charming promenade across reality"—to infinity.

## XXV

### KOHELETH AND THE CONVENTIONAL BELIEFS OF HIS AGE

After this outline of the teachings of the book, which has shown, I trust, that the thought as well as the tone of Koheleth is to be explained as a reaction against the conventional view of a world ruled by divine justice and against the current piety resulting from these views, it only remains for us to indicate the conditions under which such a book as Koheleth arose and to summarize the impression that it must have made. Apart from the evidence of language,[106] it is clear that Koheleth must have been produced at a time when religion had come to

---

[106] The Hebrew style of Koheleth is no longer the classic one of the prophets, but the later one that we find in the Mishna which, dating from the third century A.D. is that portion of the Talmud devoted to the actual laws and to which the Gemara in Aramaic represents the commentary.

mean primarily piety, an attitude of complete faith in God as conceived by the prophets and made manifest by conformity to fixed rites, centering around the temple. The synagogue or layman's temple had made its appearance but had not yet replaced the temple. Nor had the Rabbi as the lay religious teacher as yet come to the fore in place of the priest. The priest was still the official representative of the religion, but his influence was on the wane. The inconsistency involved in continuing to offer animal sacrifices to a Power of universal scope and pictured as a spiritualized ethical Force must have been pretty widely recognized, or Koheleth would not have spoken in such contemptuous terms of the futility of sacrifices and the absurdity of attributing any significance to dreams, which come through natural causes. Koheleth is probably not in advance of his times in voicing his skepticism in regard to sacrifices and to dreams. His shafts are rather directed against the *theory* of those whose piety rested in the belief in a God whose workings are described in the additions to the book—a God whom one should fear, who punishes the sinner, even though he may for a time escape retribution, who brings man to judgment for all his acts, even those which he tries to conceal, a God who has made everything good and beautiful, in whose hands are the righteous and the wise and to whom the spirit returns when death overtakes the body.

Koheleth says boldly, let us look at this theory and see whether the facts conform to it. His main

aim is to show that you cannot account for things
as they are and for the actual conditions in the
world on this theory. His book arose, therefore, in
a circle which, while it did not question the existence of God, declined to close its eyes to the difficulties involved in attempting to penetrate His
ways. It is the same circle from which the book of
Job emanated, the main difference between Job
and Koheleth being that Job takes up a particular problem—the innocent suffering in the world
—while Koheleth makes an attack upon the entire
line of the current theology. We miss the point of
both books if we regard them as purely individual
expressions. They voice views which must have
been pretty widely held, or they would not have
made a sufficiently deep impression to be the subject of subsequent elaboration and comment.
Koheleth is about a century later than Job, but
both reflect a period when independent thought
had become a factor in the intellectual life of the
day. The prophets who had brought about the
notable advance in religious thought no longer had
it all their own way. Men arose who asked the
question whether the prophets' view of life, noble
and inspiring as it was, furnished a satisfactory
explanation for the world as it actually appears.

The old opposition to prophetical Judaism on
the part of those who felt the lash of the prophets'
denunciation of Baal worship and of social corruption, had died out. The new religious com-
monwealth, organized by pious followers of Yahweh,

gradually changing to the universal Jehovah, con-
formed in theory at least to the ideals maintained
by the prophets. The worship was purged of objectionable features, and though animal sacrifices as
tribute and as expiatory offerings continued to
be the basis of the new ritualistic code worked
out under the guiding direction of Ezra, a higher
interpretation was given to the rite, as also to the
other ceremonies of the religion, growing steadily in the elaboration of details. The old abuses,
however, albeit in a different form, were beginning
to creep in. The priests as a class were again
becoming worldly. Politics became hopelessly
intertwined with the religious organization and
led to internal quarrels and intrigues. This state
of affairs was counterbalanced in a measure by
the growth of a personal piety among the laity
that found its expression in a deepening faith in a
watchful Providence, extending His care beyond
the grave, and in a punctilious ceremonialism,
such as a strict observance of the Sabbath and of
dietary laws.

Koheleth reflects clearly the two directions
towards which Judaism was drifting, a worldly
ecclesiasticism on the one hand, and personal piety
of a rather smug character on the other. The two
parties into which Judaism split, Sadduceeism,
the party of the priests, and Phariseeism, the
party of the pious laity, existed in embryo, if not
yet in definite shape. The circle from which the
book of Koheleth emanated represents the inde-

pendent line of thought, opposed to both directions in a measure, though not absolutely so. Unwilling to be bound by either tradition or convention, the circle raised the fundamental inquiry whether one can see the workings in the world of a God such as was set up by the party of tradition as well as by that of pietistic convention. The spirit of Koheleth is that of Goethe's *Geist der stets verneint*. This spirit of denial, naturally, aroused the opposition of the priests and of the pious laity alike. There is indeed something of the mephistophelian quality in Koheleth. He shares with Mephistopheles a sense of humor, though not of the same sardonic caliber. Koheleth is too sympathetic with the sufferings of mankind through the conditions prevailing in the world to indulge in mockery at man's efforts to rise superior to his surroundings. He does not question the essential soundness of human nature as a whole, and he can appreciate the earnest struggle to seek a solution for the strange contradictions in life. He manifests his pity for the struggle, which he feels, however, is hopeless because one cannot discover any real aim to human life. That is his main contention, which leads him to the conclusion that one must not take life too seriously. He, therefore, smiles at things and conditions as they are. The smile is at times benevolent, but more frequently touched with a gentle irony. He smiles at the zealous reformer who deludes himself in the belief that he can improve matters; he smiles also at the one who laments that things are growing worse. That is not so, he tells us for our comfort. The past only seems to be better because we idealize it, and in part because with the approach of old age we are apt to grow out of sympathy with the everchanging present. If there is no real progress, but merely endless repetition with variations that are unessential, there is also no retrogression. Nature has only one film—a long and varied one, which it reels off and then reels off again without cessation. Enjoy the film, he says, but don't attempt to interfere with it—or you will spoil the show.

His doctrine of enjoyment is simple and at bottom sound. Don't be a mere spectator in the drama of life or you will soon tire of it. Act your part and you will enjoy the play in which you participate by your toil so much the longer. Take life as a play, but be actor and spectator at the same time. Remember that the curtain will be rung down sometime, and you will be left in darkness. Let not this thought, however, from which, to be sure, you cannot escape, drive away your enjoyment, but resign yourself to the inevitable by the comforting assurance that the one certainty given us is the legitimacy of enjoying our leisure after the day's work. The capacity for enjoyment is a gift of God. God approves of joy, because joy is the one thing that makes life bearable.

The pessimistic note is struck by Koheleth, but it is a soft and not a harsh sound. He loves life and therefore he is not a genuine pessimist;

and when he does occasionally go beyond bounds, as when he says that he hates life, he contradicts himself in the next breath. The pessimistic mood is transitory and is generally aroused at the sad thought that the life to which he is attached must come to a close. The common fate that will over-take all rings like a refrain through the book, but it is significant that the refrain to enjoy life sounds still more strongly. His fling at woman, which might be used as an argument to prove that he is a deep-dyed pessimist, is not to be taken too seriously, any more than is his assertion in one place—and in one place only—that he hates life. One feels that he indulges in intentional exagger-ation when he declares that even among a thousand, one cannot find a decent woman. It sounded clever, and Koheleth is not the only humorist who indulges in a witty hyperbole to raise a laugh.

I call his doctrine of enjoyment sound, because he preaches joy for joy's sake. He has no sym-pathy with gluttony or riotous living, or with a life entirely given up to stimulating the passions and sensual tastes. He is saved from any extreme hedonism by his gospel of work as the condition to genuine enjoyment. Hence, when he advocates "Eat, drink, and be merry," he knows that there is little danger of making enjoyment the *aim* of life. Enjoyment as an aim is vanity and indeed the greatest of all vanities, for it must soon lead to *ennui*. He knows that even when he urges the young to follow the inclinations of their mind and the sight of their eyes, the quest for enjoyment *after* toil will go no further than to eat and drink with a merry heart, to keep oneself in a festive mood, keen for the enjoyment of one's leisure, and to live happily with one's wife and family.

It should be borne in mind in an estimate of this worldly aspect of Koheleth's philosophy that it does not differ materially from the practical wisdom frequently found in the book of Proverbs which aroused no opposition, either from the priests or from the pious laity. Poverty is looked upon in proverbs as synonymous with shame (Proverbs xiii. 18). There is a touch of cynicism in the sentiment that

> "The poor is hated even by his neighbor,
> But the rich has many friends" (xiv. 20).

The warning against the anger of kings sounds like an entry in Koheleth's diary,

> "A king's wrath is as a messenger of death.
> A wise man will pacify it" (xvi. 14).

The sentiment is the same as in Ecclesiastes (x. 4).[107] Koheleth might have given the worldly advice not to sing one's praises in the presence of a king (Proverbs xxv. 6), because it will not lead to one's advancement. Such sayings as "it is not good to eat too much honey" (xxv. 27), and "not to set one's foot too often in one's neighbor's house, lest he may tire of thee" (xxv. 17), "not to boast of to-morrow, for thou knowest not what to-morrow

---

[107] See above, p. 157.

may bring forth" (xxvii. 1), might have found a place among the "words of Koheleth." No doubt this similarity between the tone of many of Koheleth's utterances and the philistine sentiments in Proverbs was a factor in leading commentators to amplify Koheleth by sayings taken from collections of maxims. To an uncritical age, anxious, moreover, to weaken the unorthodox character of Koheleth's point of view, the device of regarding the book merely as a collection of sayings to which others bearing on the themes discussed—wisdom, the conduct of life, the value of discretion, avoidance of trouble and the like—could be added, would suggest itself as one of the means to accomplish the end in view, namely, to give the flavor of conventionalism to a popular but dangerous book.

## XXVI

### THE OMAR KHAYYAM OF THE BIBLE

Where then shall we place Koheleth among the many philosophers of earlier and later days who have set forth their attitude towards life. We have seen that he is not Mephistopheles, though he shows something of the spirit of that grim cynic. He is not a follower of Epicurus, any more than he is an adherent of Stoic philosophy. He is not unlike Lucian in his frankness and in his sense of humor. Not quite so irreverent as Lucian, he lacks the latter's biting sarcasm, but one can well understand that the more gentle cynicism of Koheleth was as distasteful to those who did not favor the disturbance of the *status quo*, as was the sharper irony in Lucian's flings at the gods as pictured in the current myths in which the intelligent public no longer believed in the second century of our era when Lucian wrote.

There are some striking points of resemblance between Koheleth and Hesiod who, reflecting the spirit of the depressing age in which he must have lived, sets forth his philosophy of life in his famous "Works and Days." Like Koheleth, Hesiod subscribes to the doctrine *Cherchez la femme*. Pandora, the type of feminine lure, is created by Zeus in punishment for Prometheus's crime of stealing fire from heaven for the benefit of mankind. She brings a box as a fatal gift to her husband Epimetheus, the brother of Prometheus, from which, upon being opened, all the ills to which human flesh is heir escape. Hope alone remains. Like Koheleth, also, Hesiod sees in work, in unceasing and unremitting labor, the only salvation for man against falling into temptation or sinking into the slough of despair in the hard "iron age" in which mankind is condemned to dwell, the age in which Honor and Justice are ever threatening to desert the world and leave it in utter misery. But Hesiod strikes a far harsher and sadder note than Koheleth. To him the successive ages of the world from the golden to the iron, represent a steadily degenerating process. Not so Koheleth, who denies that the world is any worse than it always was, though he also does not believe that it is better, nor that it can be improved. The thought, moreover, which we encounter so frequently in Greek literature, that the gods are jealous of man and fear his growing power, is entirely absent in Koheleth, though there is a suggestion of it in the more genuinely pessimistic view of mankind taken in the third chapter of Genesis. Yahweh wishes to keep man away from the Tree of Knowledge of Good and Evil and fears that he may also approach the Tree of Life and by plucking its fruit secure immortality (Genesis iii, 22). Hesiod's doctrine of work approaches more closely in fact to the view taken by the Yahwist in Genesis that toil is a curse imposed on man by an angry deity, than it does to Koheleth's view of toil as the only means of securing an enjoyment of life that will make existence bearable. To Hesiod, as to Genesis, work means, primarily, tilling of the soil. Both look upon toil as a hard task, but Hesiod tries to rise superior to the hardship and to look upon work as man's salvation. Genesis is franker in recognizing that man's life was a happier one in the golden age when he could get his sustenance without working for it in the sweat of his brow. Koheleth goes his own way and separates himself from both Hesiod and Genesis, in suggesting that the purpose of work is to save man from *ennui* and that enjoyment, coming as leisure after the heat and burden of the day, is apt to last longer and will endure at all events until the time comes when life itself ceases to be a joy and when, as described in the last chapter (xii, 3-7)—perhaps the finest in the book—strength fails and the faculties decline. "The guardians of the house"—by which Koheleth means the hips —tremble; "the grinding maidens"—the teeth —cease; "those that peer through the windows" —by which the eyes are meant—are darkened; "the sound of the mill"—the hearing—is low; and so on through the list to "the snapping of the silver cord"—the spine—and the "shattering of the golden bowl"—the brain—till at last,

"sans teeth, sans eyes, sans taste, sans everything,"

"man goes to his eternal home and the wailers go about the street." Work as long as you can, says Koheleth. Sow your seed in the morning and rest not until the evening of life comes. In this way, by enjoying also your leisure, you will get as much happiness out of life as it can furnish. Hesiod, like Koheleth, urges man to look upon work from the brighter side, but, more conventional in his attitude towards prevailing customs and beliefs, he cautions man against offending the gods by not performing prescribed rites of sacrifice and worship. On the other hand, Hesiod again joins with Koheleth in giving practical advice for the conduct of life, including the suggestion not to trust all one's goods in one venture and to live happily with one's wife and to provide for offspring— though not, he adds, in too large numbers.

Koheleth reminds one most of Omar Khayyam, who represents the natural reaction against

a stern Islamic environment, as Koheleth marks a
reaction against the unbending ecclesiasticism and
conventional piety of his Jewish surroundings.
The touch of irony in Omar Khayyam's immortal
quatrains is singularly like that which we encounter in Koheleth.

"With them the seed of Wisdom did I sow,
And with mine own hand wrought to make it grow;
And this was all the Harvest that I reap'd—
I came like Water, and like Wind I go."

In their attitude towards life, both are free from
any real bitterness. Their cynicism is without any
sting, or if occasionally there is a sting it is gentle;
it pricks a little but does not bite. Both are enam-
ored of life, despite its sorrows and its imperfections.
To both life means joy—joy for joy's sake, with
perhaps this distinction, that Omar Khayyam has
no fear of *ennui* resulting from joy, whereas Koheleth advocates as a preventive the combination of
toil with joy, so that the enjoyment may be more
lasting. The undertone of sadness, too, is common
to both, suggested by the brevity of life and by the
approach of old age, devoid of enjoyment, with the
shadow of death thrown across one's path.

"Alike for those who for To-day prepare,
And those that after some To-morrow stare,
A Muezzin from the Tower of Darkness cries:
'Fools! your Reward is neither Here nor There.'"

Both writers are worldly in their spirit and their
outlook; and this is the severest indictment—if it
be one—to be preferred against their productions.

*Carpe diem!* is the motto of Koheleth and of Omar Khayyam alike.

> "Come, fill the Cup, and in the fire of Spring
> Your Winter-garment of Repentance fling;
> The Bird of Time has but a little way
> To flutter—and the Bird is on the Wing."

Let us be frank and recognize that there is no spiritual uplift—to use a term that is much over-worked in modern days—in Koheleth, as little as in the Islamic poet. Koheleth in its original form was not a religious book, and had no place in a sacred canon. It lacks edification, so essential to a religious production. But neither is it irreligious, as the pious commentators believed who tried to give to Koheleth's utterances an orthodox turn. Koheleth is not a scoffer, and he is certainly not atheistically inclined. He takes the existence of God for granted. He has thrown off the beliefs common to all Semites and indeed to all peoples in an early stage of culture, who, because unable to conceive of life coming to a complete stop, imagined a great gathering place where the dead lie conscious but inactive, but he has not advanced to any faith in a real immortality. In this respect, however, he stands on the same grade as the Sadducees, who because of their conservatism likewise did not accept the more advanced doctrine. Koheleth draws the consequences of the position held by him, and, no longer accepting the view that any consciousness remains to the dead, boldly says that "They know nothing" (ix. 4). Death ends every-

thing. It was this attitude that was largely responsible for the opposition that the book encountered
in Pharisaic circles, where opposing views of a retribution in another world for one's acts in this one
are reflected in the additions to the book. We
must bear in mind however, in defending Koheleth
from the charge of being irreligious, that even the
Psalmist declares when praying for a prolongation
of life that the dead cannot praise God in Sheol
(Psalms vi. 6). The author of Job, likewise, does
not stress the belief in immortality, even though
he may not specifically have denied it. Job's longing for the grave,

"Where the wicked cease from troubling
And the weary are at rest" (iii. 17),

suggests no distinction between the fate of the
just and that of the wicked, as little as it leaves
place for any consciousness—certainly not for any
happiness—beyond the portals of this world.

It may be claimed that the general attitude
of mind of Koheleth betokens an irreligious spirit.
Perhaps—from the orthodox and pietistic point of
view; and it must be admitted that his advice,
objectionable also from the standpoint of ethics
—"not to be overrighteous" (vii. 16)—may be in-
stanced as a proof of his lack of religious reverence.
Outbalancing such an utterance, however, is his
sympathy with those who suffer injustice and with
those who perish because of human ingratitude.
Such sympathy is typical of a religiously inclined
disposition. We might go so far as to say that

mistic mood—smile at the world, not with a bitter smile, but with a suggestion of irony.

Renan, whose own nature found a response in Koheleth and who was fascinated by the book as everyone must be who penetrates its spirit, goes so far as to say that it is the only amiable book written by a Jew. That is hardly correct, for we have a modern analogy to Koheleth (as Renan himself suggests) in Heine, who looks upon the world in the same smiling manner. While thoroughly assimilating the culture and surroundings of his age, Heine's humor and general type of mind are characteristically Jewish. Heine is a nineteenth-century Koheleth; and he posesses the same irresistible charm. His pen, though trenchant, is never dipped in venom; his irony, though pointed, is tempered with pathos. Even his satire, when most biting, betrays his amiability. The analogy between the two might be carried further, for their skepticism is much of the same order: they are both "gentle cynics." We can imagine Koheleth as he bids farewell to the world, and in the contemplation of his life recalls, perhaps, the utterances in his book which offended the orthodox and the pious, murmuring with a smile on his dying lips, as did Heine, "*Dieu me pardonnera—c'est son métier.*"

EXPLANATORY NOTE:—The translation follows the original text, as restored in accordance with the principles laid down in the preceding discussion. All additions, as well as comments and glosses, are relegated to the footnotes; and in order that the reader may obtain a connected survey of these amplifications to the original book of Koheleth, they have been grouped in the appendix under three divisions: (1) The additions made by the pious commentators with a view of converting Koheleth into a book acceptable to Jewish orthodoxy; (2) the maxims added in large numbers to give the book the character of a collection of sayings for the guidance of life, like the Book of Proverbs and the Wisdom of Ben Sira (*i.e.*, Ecclesiasticus); and (3) miscellaneous comments, glosses and minor changes introduced into the text.

The translation, disregarding the late divisions into chapters in our Bibles, has been divided into 24 sections, each section covering some aspect of the theme, with the conclusions drawn by Koheleth from his arguments and observations. A general heading for each section has been added on the margin. For the sake of convenience, and in order to facilitate a comparison of the translation with the Book of Koheleth as given in our Bibles, the chapter and verses in the Bible version, corresponding to each section, are likewise placed on the margin and—as a further guide—so that the reader may see at a glance the omissions in my translation, the number of the verse *preceding* and that of the verse *following* an omission are likewise added on the margin. A letter after a verse number indicates a part of that verse, thus $1^a$ means the first part of the verse, $1^b$ the second part, while $1^c$ is the third part in the case of a long verse, divided into three obvious parts, and $1^d$ a fourth part. In the case of brief insertions, I have not considered it necessary to indicate this on the margin, but all such insertions have been noted in the footnotes.

# THE WORDS OF KOHELETH[1]

## I

What gain has a man of all his toil,[2]
Which he toils under the sun?[3]
Generation comes and generation goes,
But the earth remains forever.
The sun rises and the sun sets,
And to his rising place he returns.[4]
Around to the south and circling to the north,
Around and around goes the wind,
And on its circuits the wind returns.[5]

*i. 3-11
The
Eternal Cycle
in Life and
Nature, with-
out Goal
or Progress.*

---

[1] The heading in our Bibles (i. 1) "The words of Koheleth (son of David) a King in Jerusalem" represents a late addition. The Hebrew construction, moreover, shows that the words "son of David" have been superimposed upon the heading after the tradition had been established which identified Koheleth with Solomon, "the son of David." The superimposed words are, therefore, in the nature of a gloss or comment. See further above, p. 66. The summary (i. 2) that follows the heading

"Vanity of vanities, says Koheleth, vanity of vanities, all is vanity"

is likewise a late insertion taken over from the end of the book (xii. 8), with "vanity of vanities" repeated, either for the sake of emphasis or as a general superscription to the book.

[2] The first nine verses (i. 3–11), consisting of two sections (1) verses 3–8 (poetic in form) and (2) verses 9–11 (prose) are in the nature of an introduction. This introduction may be regarded as a general summary of the teachings of the book, which properly opens with verse 12. The introduction was added after the book had been written, and it *may* be the work of someone who shared the views of Koheleth and tried his hand at making an addition to the book. At the same time, while the possibility of this view, held by

201

All streams flow into the sea,
But the sea is not full.
To the place whither the streams flow,
From there they flow back again.[6]
Everything is wearied,
Beyond human utterance,[7]

---

some scholars, may be admitted, the tone and language of the introduction are so completely in the manner of Koheleth, that it seems preferable in the absence of any decisive evidence to the contrary, to include it as an integral part of the work. I so regard it with all the less hesitation, because of the difficulty of assuming the existence of a writer who could imitate Koheleth so successfully and produce such a literary gem as this picture of the perpetual repetition in the domain of nature.

[3] The picturesque expression "under the sun" occurs no less than 30 times in the book. It is, therefore, a characteristic phrase of our author, who prefers it to the more prosaic and conventional "upon the earth" (viii. 14, 16 and xi. 2). By the side of "under the sun," we also find three times the phrase "under heaven" (i. 13, ii. 3 and iii. 1), though "heaven" (written in Hebrew *sh-m-m*) may be a copyist's slip in these passages for "sun" (written *sh-m-sh*).

[4] My translation of this line rests upon a slight textual change and involves also taking one word as an explanation of a rarer one. The thought is that the sun never reaches any goal, though always appearing to be moving towards one.

[5] It comes back to the direction whence it started. The wind, too, has no goal.

[6] The view rests upon the theory, widely held in antiquity, that there was an ocean encircling the earth, upon which the earth floated like a rubber ball. Rivers and lakes and springs were supposed to be fed by subterranean streams, connecting with the great encircling ocean. The streams likewise have no goal; they simply flow forward and backward.

[7] This *monotony* of regular changes without any goal makes life so wearisome that speech fails one in trying to describe it.

Beyond sight and hearing.[8]
What has been is that which shall be;
And what has happened is that which shall
    happen,
So that there is nothing new under the sun.

If something (occurs) of which one says, "See,
this is new"—ages before us it has already happened. Former occurrences are not recorded, and
later occurrences also shall not be remembered by
the ages that are to come.

## II

I, Koheleth, was king over Israel in Jerusalem, i. 12-ii. 11.
and I applied my mind[9] to seek and explore[10] every- *The*
thing under the sun[10a]—a sorry business which *Vanity of Pleasures.*
God[11] has given the children of men for [their]
affliction.[12] I saw all that happened under the sun i. 14

---

[8] Literally: "The eye is not satisfied with seeing and
the ear is not filled through hearing," *i.e.*, no matter how
much one sees and how much one hears, one cannot exhaust
the impression of the utter wearisomeness of the processes
of nature. Nature herself grows tired and weary of this
perpetual movement without progress.

[9] The Hebrew word is "heart," but the heart was supposed by the Hebrews (and other peoples of antiquity) to be
the seat of the "intellect." Hence, wherever the word "heart"
occurs in the O.T., the mind is meant.

[10] "Through wisdom," added by a commentator to
conform to the Solomon of tradition.

[10a] Text has "heaven," but this is probably a slip for "sun."

[11] Koheleth always uses the generic name for the deity—
Elohim—never the specifically Hebrew one, Yahweh. He does
not write from the Hebrew point of view. See above p. 134.

[12] The desire for knowledge, implanted in man, is a
cause of trouble and vexation. The word rendered "busi-

—and behold it was all vanity and chasing after wind.[13]

i. 16　　Now I thought to myself,[14] I have become great and acquired much more[15] than any one who reigned before me over Jerusalem, and my mind was stored with very much wisdom and knowledge.

i. 17　　And so I set out to experience frivolity and foolishness,[16] though I knew that this, too, was chasing after wind.[17]

---

ness" (or we might say "task" or "occupation") occurs *only* in Ecclesiastes—and no less than eight times. The point of view is much the same that we find in the famous third chapter of Genesis, which likewise assumes that the evil in the world is due to man's desire for knowledge. The state of blissful ignorance before man ate of the "Tree of Knowledge of Good and Evil" was Paradise. See above p. 188.

[13] A very striking phrase, occurring nine times in the book, to indicate the utter foolishness of it all. Life is an empty bubble. Ambition is like chasing the wind. You can never catch it, and if you did it would be of no use. At this point (i. 15), a commentator added a popular saying:

"The crooked cannot be straightened,
And the lacking cannot be supplied."

This interrupts the context and introduces an entirely different thought, namely, that things cannot be changed. See vii. 13.

[14] Literally: "I spoke with my heart" (*i.e.*, my mind).

[15] A commentator adds "wisdom," to make the description conform to the traditional Solomon, but Koheleth here has in mind material possessions.

[16] A pious editor, who thought that this was a bit too strong and hardly consistent with the traditional figure of a wise Solomon, added "wisdom and knowledge," though these words are manifestly out of place. The point made by the author is that Koheleth *after* having acquired "wisdom and knowledge" (in addition to possessions), and finding that this was "vanity and chasing after wind," now determined

I said to myself, come I'll make a test of <sup>ii. 1</sup> pleasure and of having a good time,[18] but alas! This also turned out to be vanity. Of sport, I was led to conclude that it was madness, and of joy—what does it accomplish! I made up my mind to stimulate my body with wine[19] and to pursue folly, in order to ascertain whether this was a good way for the children of men to spend[19a] the days of their lives.

I undertook great works. I acquired me houses; I planted me vineyards, I made me gardens and parks.[20] I planted in them all kinds of fruit trees,[21]

---

to see what the antithesis of "wisdom and knowledge", *i.e.*, "frivolity and foolishness," would lead to.

[17] A glossator, perhaps not the same as the one who interspersed the book with proverbial sayings (see above p. 76), here added (i. 18.)

> " For in much wisdom is much trouble,
>   And increase of knowledge is increase of pain."

This saying (verse 18) properly belongs after verse 14.

[18] Literally "looking upon good"—a perfect equivalent to our colloquial "having a good time." Koheleth is not afraid of using the expressive slang of his day.

[19] At this point a pious commentator, still concerned for the reputation of the good and wise king, added "though my mind was acting with wisdom," *i.e.*, the king kept control of himself. It would not do to represent Solomon as a wine bibber, led by his sensual taste to pass beyond bounds. He was merely experimenting and with a conscious purpose.

[19a] A glossator adds "under heaven," but this is quite superfluous, and besides appears to be a slip for "under the sun." See note 3.

[20] The word is the Persian *pairidaêza*, literally an "enclosure," which passed over into Greek as *Paradeisos*. Outside of this passage, it occurs only twice in the O.T. (1) Song of Songs iv. 13 and (2) Neh. ii. 8—both books belonging to the post-Persian period.

I made me pools of water to irrigate the sprouting forest.[22]   I purchased slaves and hand-maidens, and had a household of dependents, besides having possessions of cattle and flocks in large number, more than anyone before me in Jerusalem.   I gathered me also silver and gold, royal treasures and provinces,[23] I got me singers and dancing maidens[24] and [all] the delights of the children of men.[25]

And so I became great,[26] in excess of any one who was before me in Jerusalem.[27]   I did not withhold anything that my eyes desired, I did not deny myself any pleasure, for I rejoiced in all my toil, and this was my portion of all my toil.   But when I looked on all what my hands had wrought and on what I had toiled for—all indeed seemed vanity and chasing after wind.   Nothing seemed worth while[28] under the sun.

---

[21] With an allusion to the primæval garden (Gen. ii. 9) with all kinds of trees.

[22] A commentator adds "of trees."

[23] Instead of "provinces," Ehrlich (Randglossen, Vol. vii. 61) by a slight textual change, obtains the word "choice treasures" which forms a suitable parallel to "royal treasures."   However, the text as it stands gives a satisfactory meaning, in view of Solomon's extension of his kingdom.

[24] Literally, "male and female singers."

[25] Two obscure terms are added, commonly taken as "many concubines," but it seems more likely that they were intended as variants to "singers and dancing maidens"; and, not being understood, they were incorrectly spelled.

[26] Note the sarcastic touch, that the greatness of kings consists in having large possessions and in surrounding themselves with luxuries, slaves and courtesans.

## III

And so I made a test of madness and folly,[29] for what can any man do who comes after a king, beyond what he has already done?[30] And yet it seemed to me that perhaps wisdom *has* an advantage over folly, in so far as light is better than darkness.[31] But then I realized that there is one and the same fate for all; and I reflected that the fate of the fool will also overtake me. Why then should I be overwise? So I concluded—this, also, is vanity. For of the wise man, as of the fool, there is no permanent record, inasmuch as in the days to come everything is forgotten.[32] And [see] how the wise man dies just as the fool!

*ii. 12- 16*
*Wisdom and Folly Equally Vain.*

*ii. 14ᵇ*

---

[27] Our pious commentator again adds, "However, my wisdom abided with me." Solomon *must* be represented as keeping wise through it all.

[28] Literally: "advantage." The word used occurs only in Ecclesiastes, though a favorite one with our author, who introduces it no less than nine times. It seems to be a colloquial expression, equivalent to our "worth while."

[29] Our pious commentator to conform to the Solomonic tradition again adds "and wisdom."

[30] The experiment made by Koheleth is final, for surely no one can make a more complete test of pleasure, wealth and riotous living than a king. There is also an implied sarcasm that no one can possibly be more foolish than a king.

[31] The commentator, who intersperses appropriate proverbs throughout the book, adds:

"The wise man has his eyes in his head,
But the fool walks in darkness." (Verse 14ª.)

[32] It is interesting to contrast with this the point of view in Proverbs x. 7: "The memory of the righteous shall be blessed, but the name of the wicked shall rot." Similarly Psalm cxii. 6 "The righteous shall be in everlasting remembrance."

## IV

ii. 17-25
*Life is*
*Hateful and*
*Toil is*
*Useless—*
*Therefore*
*Eat, Drink,*
*and be*
*Merry!*

So I hated life, for all that happened under the sun seemed evil to me, since all was vanity and chasing after wind. And I hated [the thought] that I must leave all that I had toiled for under the sun, to one who comes after me. And who knows whether he who will control all that I have toiled for under the sun with my wisdom will be a wise man or a fool? Surely this is vanity!

And I gave myself up to despair over all that I had toiled for under the sun, inasmuch as a man who toils with wisdom, knowledge and integrity[33] must hand it over as an inheritance to one who has not toiled for it—surely this is vanity and a great evil.[34]

What has a man of all his toil and of his painstaking efforts under the sun, since all his days are pains and his ambition a vexation, with no rest for his mind even at night? Surely this is vanity.

There is nothing better for a man than to eat and to drink and to enjoy himself for his toil; and it indeed seems to me that such is the will of God.[35]

---

[33] Again a word used only in Koheleth (occurring three times), and which represents either a late formation or a colloquial expression.

[34] Koheleth betrays a very "modern" point of view in thus railing against the law of inheritance, which obliges a man to leave his property to his children who have not worked for it.

[35] Literally: "This is from the hand of God," *i.e.*, enjoyment is sanctioned by the divine fiat. The capacity to enjoy is God's gift to man. The same thought is found in iii. 13, and v. 19 and forms an essential part of Koheleth's philosophy. See p. 147.

For who should eat and who should drink,[36] apart
from him,[37] though this, also, is vanity and chasing
after wind.[38]

### V

Everything has its appointed time,[39] and
there is a time [determined] for every occurrence
under the sun.[39a]

iii. 1-15
*Everything
is Pre-
ordained—*

> There is a time [appointed] to be born, and a
>     time to die.
>
> There is a time [appointed] for planting, and
>     a time for uprooting.[40]

iii. 2

---

[36] I follow the Greek text in preference to the Hebrew,
which has an obscure word, that may rest upon a misreading.

[37] Who is to enjoy the products of the earth if not man?
I follow the Greek translation reading "him," instead of the
Hebrew "I."

[38] The pious commentator who aims to tone down the
cynical conclusion, which is particularly distasteful to him,
adds (ii. 26):

> "For to the man who is good in His sight, He (*i.e.*, God) has given
> wisdom and knowledge and enjoyment, but to the sinner He has
> assigned the task of gathering and amassing, in order to hand it over
> to the one who is good in the sight of God."

This is optimism with a vengeance, and in complete contrast
to Koheleth's philosophy. See above, p. 137, *et seq.* It is
amusing to follow the mental antics of some exegetes in their
endeavor to reconcile the two points of view—the one absolutely exclusive of the other.

[39] The word used occurs only in late books of the O. T.

[39a] So read instead of "heaven." See note 3.

[40] Some elaborator has amused himself—or perhaps
several hands are to be assumed—by adding a somewhat
tiresome series of 12 further antitheses (verses 3-8), in illustration of the general principle of a time being preordained
for all occurrences, as laid down by Koheleth. Some of these
antitheses are appropriate, others are far-fetched and a few

iii. 9    What profit, then, has the worker of his toil?[41]
I have observed [every] ambition[42] which God
has given the children of men for their affliction.[43]
He has given them a grasp of the whole world,[44]

---

are banal.    Koheleth was too much of a literary artist to
weaken his thought by an over supply of illustrations.

> (1) A time to destroy, and a time to repair.
> (2) A time to break down, and a time to build up.
> (3) A time to weep, and a time to laugh.
> (4) A time to mourn, and a time to dance.
> (5) A time to scatter stones, and a time to gather stones.
> (6) A time to embrace, and a time to refrain from embracing.
> (7) A time to seek, and a time to give up as lost.
> (8) A time to keep, and a time to throw away.
> (9) A time to rip, and a time to sew.
> (10) A time to keep silent, and a time to speak.
> (11) A time to love, and a time to hate.
> (12) A time of war, and a time of peace.

It will be observed that the 3d and 4th of these antitheses are
practically synonymous, as are the 2nd and 5th and 9th, and
again the 7th and 8th. Some like the 6th and 11th are rather
trivial, or at all events entirely too obvious to be worthy of a
place in a book like Koheleth.    The list impresses one as an
attempted *jeu d'esprit*, to see how many antitheses might be
suggested.   We ought to be grateful that the list was not further extended, as it might easily have been.    It would also
appear that the one (or those) who added these illustrations
lost sight of Koheleth's thought of predetermination and
took "time" to mean the *proper* time, instead of the *fixed* time.

[41] Koheleth's thought is, that everything is preordained
and the time for its occurrence fixed.   Why then toil and
worry?   Things will happen anyway at the appointed time.

[42] The same word as above, i. 13 ("business") of
which our author is so fond.   The Greek text adds "every"
which is proper at this point.

[43] The pious commentator interposes a counter-reflec-
tion (iii. 11ᵃ), "He has made everything beautiful in its
season," with an allusion perhaps to the refrain in the first
chapter of Genesis, "And God saw that it was good."

[44] Literally: "He has placed the [whole] world in their

without, however, the possibility on the part of man to fathom the work which God has made from the beginning to the end.

I realized, therefore, that there is nothing better for a man than to be happy and to enjoy himself,[45] in his life, and that indeed every man who eats and drinks and has a good time in all his toil [enjoys] a gift of God.[46] I [also] realized that whatever God does is forever, to which one cannot add and from which one cannot take away.[47] Whatever has been has been before, and what is to be has already been.[48]

---

mind," meaning that God has given men a grasp on the world. The Greek text adds "whole" to "world" which shows that the Hebrew word here used, ōlām, originally, "forever," had acquired the meaning "world," common in post-Biblical Hebrew.

[45] The text says "to do good," but that is surely not what Koheleth has in mind. Either the phrase has also the force of to "get pleasure," or it is an intentional correction of the phrase "to look upon good" which is the one that Koheleth generally uses (e.g., ii. 1 and 24) to express the idea of "having a good time."

[46] i.e., It is God's will—as above ii. 24.

[47] God's work is permanent, just as He has made it. Man cannot add to it or take away from it. Why, therefore, be ambitious to direct affairs into their proper channel? The pious commentator adds, "God has so made it (i.e., the world) that men will fear Him."

[48] The same thought as in i. 9. Then follows what appears to be an addition on the part of a pious commentator (15[b]) "And God seeks out what has been driven away," by which apparently is meant that God looks out for those who are rejected or persecuted, and that nothing worth preserving is lost in this world—a pious and conventional thought hardly in keeping with Koheleth's point of view.

*iii. 16-22*
*Injustice and the Common Fate.*
*iii. 18*

And furthermore, I saw under the sun in the place of justice wickedness, and where the righteous should have been the wicked was.[49] [And] I reflected that God [permits this] in the case of children of men to test them and to show that they are—beasts.[50] For the fate of the children of men and the fate of the beast is the same. As this one dies, so is the death of that, and there is the same spirit[51] to all. Man has no advantage over the beast, for all is vanity. All go to one place. All are of the dust and all return to dust.[52]

---

[49] *i.e.*, a topsy-turvy world, where things are just the contrary of what they ought to be. Our pious commentator, shocked at this picture of perversion in a world supposed to be under the government of a just God, adds, in imitation of the style of Koheleth (verse 17), "But I reflected that God will judge both the righteous and the wicked, for there *is* an appointed time for every occurrence and for every [fixed] act." The commentator thus rather cleverly turns Koheleth's view of preordination against him. A supercommentator has added "fixed." The Greek text omits the word, but it is a proper explanation to the word "time" to which it perhaps belongs.

[50] Koheleth ironically introduces the stock argument of the pious conservatives—as in the book of Job—that God allows injustice, in order to test the caliber of men. Oh yes, says Koheleth, to test them but with what result? To find out that they are—simply beasts, on a par with the animal world. At the end of verse 18, there is a gloss "they to them" —probably misplaced and belonging to verse 19, to explain that men are like beasts in having the same fate.

[51] Literally: "breath," used in Hebrew to convey the idea of both life and the soul.

[52] Almost a literal quotation from Genesis iii. 19:
"Dust thou art and unto dust shalt thou return."
The book of Koheleth thus assumes the existence of the Book of Genesis in its final form.

Who knows whether the spirit of the children of men mounts up[53] and the spirit of the beast goes down?[54] So it appeared to me that there is nothing better for man than to enjoy himself, for that is his portion, for who can help him to see what shall be after him?[55]

## VII

And once more I considered all the oppressions practised under the sun, and Oh, the tears of the oppressed without any one to console[56] them, and the violence of their oppressors with no comforter[57] in sight! And I praised those long since dead more than those still living; and better than both is the one who has not yet been, inasmuch as he has not seen the evil happenings under the sun.[58]

*iv. 1-8*
*Oppression and the Vanity of Effort.*

And I considered that all toil and all honest[59] work is merely due to man's zeal against his

*iv. 4*

---

[53] An interesting indication of the existence at the time of the composition of Koheleth of at least the beginnings of the belief which placed the seat of the dead in the heavens, as against the earlier view among all Semites which assumed a large gathering-place for all the dead—good and bad alike—in the hollow of the earth. See above, p. 129 *et seq.* and Jastrow "Hebrew and Babylonian Traditions," chapter iv.

[54] An explanatory gloss adds "to the earth."

[55] The future is hidden behind a veil, which no one can lift.

[56] In the sense of avenging them.

[57] *i.e.*, no avenger.

[58] A similar thought is expressed in the famous passage in Job iii. 11-17. By way of contrast, and voicing the optimism of the pious believer, the Psalmist (cxv. 17-18) praises the living who can sing to Yahweh, whereas "the dead praise not Yahweh" and are therefore to be pitied.

[59] The same late term as used above, ii. 21 ("integrity") to indicate a sincere and properly carried out task.

iv. 6 neighbor—surely this is vanity and chasing after wind.[60] Better a handful in quiet than two handsful in toil and chasing after wind.[61]

iv. 8 And I further considered the vanity that there is under the sun. There is a single man without a mate,[62] without a son or brother, yet toiling without end, and with an eye never satisfied by his wealth. For whom then should I toil and deprive myself of a good time? Surely this is vanity and a sorry business.[63]

## VIII

iv. 13-16
*Vanity of Youth and of Popularity.*

Better is a child of humble birth[64] and wise than an old king who is a fool and unable to take

[60] This rather cynical reflection that even honest work done by man is prompted merely by his keen desire to outdo his neighbor, leads the "maxim" commentator to add a popular proverb to illustrate the superiority of work over idleness—which is exactly what Koheleth did *not* mean.

"The fool folds his hands and consumes his own flesh." (iv. 5.) The thought is in accord with the point of view in Proverbs vi. 10; xix. 24; xxiv. 33, etc.—quite conventional.

[61] This saying *may* have been added by some commentator, but it is so appropriate to Koheleth's thought that the point must not be pressed. I, therefore, retain it as part of the original work, just as in the case of the saying (ix. 4),

"As a living dog, one is better off than a dead lion"

where Koheleth himself, without much doubt, quotes a familiar proverb.

[62] Was Koheleth an old bachelor? There seems to be an autobiographical touch here, especially in the question with which the verse ends.

[63] Some commentator takes up the point in a much more serious sense than Koheleth intended and tells us at length (iv. 9-12)

"Two are better than one,
for they secure a better return for their toil."

care of himself.[65] For through a rebellion[66] one may come to rule, even though one is born poor in one's own kingdom.

I saw all the living[67] under the sun flocking to the side of the child, who[68] was to stand in his[69] place. There was no end to all the people,[70] yet those that come after will not rejoice in him—now surely this is vanity and chasing after wind.

> In case they fall [*i.e.*, if they fail in business], the one can lift his fellow up,
> but if a single person falls, there is none to lift him up.
> Again, if two sleep together [the reference is to marriage] they keep warm,
> but how can a single person keep warm?
> And if some one attacks, there are two to withstand;
> and a triple cord is not easily snapped,"

*i.e.*, when three get twisted up in a mêlée, there is little danger of the two who stick together being worsted. At the worst, such a struggle ends in a draw.

[64] The term used is *misken* which, through the Arabic, has passed over into European languages (French *mesquin*) reverts to the Babylonian *mushkenu*, which designates a "plebeian."

[65] So Ehrlich's happy interpretation of the phrase used.

[66] Literally: "house of rebellion" in the sense of "conspiracy". This is more probable than "prison house" in the ordinary translations. See Barton's commentary, p. 121.

[67] *i.e.*, all the people.

[68] The text adds the words "the second," which is a misplaced gloss and belongs to verse 10 as an explanation of "the one," who lifts his fallen partner up.

[69] *i.e.*, in place of the deposed king.

[70] The text adds as a note to "all," *i.e.*, "before whom he was." The point is that those who once stood by the old king now rush to follow the popular youth, rising from his humble station to the kingdom, but even this popularity will not last. Those who come later, when this young king will have grown old, will not care for him. There is a reference here to some actual occurrence, from which Koheleth drew his lesson.

iv. 17–v. 6
*Vanity of*      Observe thy pilgrimages[71] to the house of
*Worship,* God but draw nigh to hear, rather than to have
*of Sacrifice* fools[72] offer a sacrifice, for they do not know
*and of* enough to do any harm.
*Vows.*

v. 1      Be not rash with thy mouth, and be not led
hastily to utter a word before God, for God is in
v. 3ᵃ heaven and thou art upon earth. Therefore, let
thy words be few.[73] If thou *dost* make a vow to God,
do not defer paying it.[74] Whatever thou vowest,
v. 4 pay! It is better not to vow, than to vow and not
pay. Let not thy mouth bring sin upon thee,[75] and
do not say before God[76] that it was a slip.[77] Why

---

[71] A reference to the three festivals during the year, when it was customary for those living outside of Jerusalem to pay a visit to the temple.

[72] By "fools," Koheleth in most uncomplimentary fashion means the priests. If you go to a place of worship, go to listen to a sermon and not to see the priests offer an animal sacrifice, as though this were pleasing to God. From Koheleth's advanced point of view, animal sacrifice is a silly survival and those who carry it out are fools. A misplaced gloss (in verse 3) adds "for He [*i.e.*, God] has no pleasure in fools." See above, p. 153, *et seq.*

[73] Don't make too many vows, and be careful before you promise anything in the house of worship when you are supposed to be in God's presence. Verse 2 interrupts the context. It belongs to verse 6. See below, note 79.

[74] The text adds, "for He has no pleasure in fools," which is a misplaced gloss, evidently a comment on the part of one who sympathized with Koheleth's characterization of priests as fools (iv. 17). See above, note 72.

[75] *i.e.*, by hastily making a vow which you have no intention to pay.

[76] So the Greek text, for which the Hebrew in order to avoid the anthropomorphism has "angel," *i.e.*, a messenger

arouse God's anger[78] and destroy thy own handiwork?

> A multitude of dreams results in many foolish
>     words,
> for a dream comes through too much business,
> and a fool's voice is heard in many words. [79]

### X

If thou seest the oppression of the poor, and
justice and righteousness in the country[80] de-
frauded, do not be amazed at the occurence, for

*v. 7-8*
*Corruption of*
*Government.*

---

of God. This substitute is quite frequent in the O.T. So,
*e.g.*, Genesis xlviii. 16, Jacob is made to speak of "the angel
who redeemed me," meaning Yahweh. In accordance with
this tendency to avoid the earlier assumption that Yahweh
*himself* appears and speaks, later documents—like the Elohist in the Hexateuch—speak of the "angel of Yahweh"
appearing in a dream or in a theophany. So Genesis xxviii. 12
the angels of God appear to Jacob in a dream, whereas in an
earlier document, which has been dovetailed into a later
one, Yahweh himself appears and speaks (verse 13).

[77] The word used is the technical one in the ritual laws
of the Pentateuch for an "unintentional error." It is peculiar
to the late Priestly Code and points, therefore, to the existence of this Code at the time that Koheleth wrote. This of
itself would bring the composition of our book to a date later
than the close of the fifth century.

[78] Literally: "Why should God be angry at thy voice,"
*i.e.*, at thee?

[79] I combine verse 6 with verse 2. The fool's voice is
that of the one who pretends to interpret a dream, which is
merely due to having too much on one's mind. Koheleth
might have added "or too much in one's stomach." At the
close of verse 6 the pious commentator adds "but fear God."

[80] The word used (*medinā*=province) is a late one and
stamps Palestine as a "province" of the Persian Empire.

there is some "guardian"[81] higher up and still higher ones above this one; and overtopping them all is the King.[82]

## XI

v. 9-16
*Vanity of Wealth.*

He who loves silver will never have enough silver,
and he who loves a big pile, will have no
    profit [of it]—
surely this is vanity.
With the increase of goods, its participants
    increase;
and what advantage is it to its owner except
    to look at it?
Sweet is the sleep of the laborer, whether he
    has eaten little or much,
but the satiety of the rich does not permit
    him to sleep.[83]
A sore evil that I have seen under the sun, is

v. 13 riches hoarded by the owner,[84] and when that for-

---

[81] Koheleth uses the word "guardian," *i.e.*, of the law, ironically. His point is that if there is graft in the land, there is always some one "higher up" who is responsible and who cannot be reached.

[82] This translation of verse 8 is a mere venture. The text as it stands cannot be correct. The two words at the close "attached to the field" give no sense whatsoever, and may represent a misplaced gloss to "laborer" in v. 11 to indicate that the "laborer" meant is a farmer. The previous verse suggests some such meaning as that responsibility for corruption in the final analysis rests with the king who stands above all. It is not improbable that the text has been intentionally manipulated for fear of *lèse-majesté*.

[83] These two lines form a popular saying, but probably introduced by Koheleth himself.

[84] A gloss adds "to his hurt."

tune is lost through a bad venture, the son begotten by him has nothing.

He cannot carry anything that he has acquired *v. 14ᵇ* by his toil away with him.[85] Surely this *is* a sore evil, that just as he came, so he goes. Therefore, what profit is it to him that he toils for the wind and that he spends all his days in saving[86] and in constant worry and sickness and distress?

## XII

Therefore, it seems to me the thing that is *v. 17-19* good and proper is to eat, drink, and to have a *Eat,* good time with all one's toil under the sun during *Drink,* the span of life which God has allotted to one, for *and be* that is his portion. Every man to whom God has *Merry.* given riches and possessions and who has [also] the power to enjoy it and to take his portion and to be happy in his toil—this is a gift of God.[87] For he should remember that life is short and that God approves of joy.[88]

---

[85] Our "maxim" commentator adds (at the beginning of verse 14) as appropriate at this point:

"As he came naked from his mother's womb, so he returns as he came."

The saying is identical with Job i. 20—there put into the mouth of Job. It is, in all probability, intended as a quotation, though placed in the third person as against the first person in Job.

[86] So by a slight change in the text.

[87] As above ii. 24.

[88] Literally: "God answers the joy of his heart"— evidently meaning that God puts his stamp of approval on man's enjoyment of his life. This use of "answer" in the sense of "approve" is also found in Arabic and Assyrian.

## XIII

vi. 1-9
*Vanity of
Life without
Enjoyment.*

There is an evil which I have observed under the sun and it bears heavily on mankind—a man to whom God has given riches and possessions and superfluity[89] with nothing lacking of anything that he might wish for, but to whom God has not given the power to enjoy it, so that a stranger[90] enjoys it—this surely is vanity and a sore evil.

If a man beget a hundred children[91] and live many years, be his life ever so long, and he does not get his fill of joy out of it[92]—I say that the abortion is happier than he. Even though it [the untimely birth] comes into vanity, moves in darkness, and with darkness its name is covered and it has never seen the sun nor has known [anything]—

vi. 6 yet this is preferable to the other.[93] And though a man live a thousand years twice told, and has not had a good time—do not all go to one place?[94]

[89] Literally "honor," but when used with "riches" it has the force of luxury.

[90] *i.e.,* some one for whom he does not care. Is Koheleth again giving us an autobiographical touch of himself as a bachelor who must leave his fortune to strangers?

[91] Grandchildren and great-grandchildren would also be counted as a man's offspring.

[92] A glossater has added "And he has not even a burial," *i.e.,* is even neglected when he dies. The common view among Semites was that the unburied corpse is unhappy in the world of shadows.

[93] *i.e.,* the fate of the untimely birth is better than a long life without joy, even if one has children to whom to leave one's fortune.

[94] According to Koheleth, there is no heaven for the good man who has lived his life in abstinence and whose

What advantage has a wise man[95] over a fool, vi. 8
or the poor man who by his knowledge sets an example to the living?[96] Better is enjoyment[97] than
longing—though this also is vanity and chasing
after wind.

### XIV

Whatever is has long since been determined[98] vi. 10-12
and what man is has been fixed.[99] He cannot con- *Vanity*
tend with what is stronger than himself.[100] Since *of the*<br>*Struggle*
many possessions[101] merely increase vanity, what *against Fate.*

energy was entirely taken up with toil without cessation.
His fate is no better than that of the man who lived solely
for enjoyment. A "maxim" commentator has added a
popular saying at this point as an antidote to Koheleth's
poisonous doctrine of eating and drinking and jollification
as the goal and aim of life (v. 7)—

> "All the toil of a man is for his mouth [*i.e.*, for his belly],
>     and yet the appetite is never satisfied."

[95] The wise man being here as elsewhere also the good man,
and by implication the one who lives to work and not to enjoy.

[96] My translation of the close of verse 8 is a guess at
the meaning of an obscure phrase.

[97] Literally: "sight [*i.e.*, feasting] of the eyes." This
saying *may* also be an insertion by the "maxim" commentator, though it is in keeping with Koheleth's tone and thought.

[98] Literally: "its name has been called." The "giving
of a name" according to Semitic ideas is equivalent to calling
something into existence. The phrase, therefore, means
that whatever is has been brought into existence long before
it actually appears, *i.e.*, things are preordained.

[99] Every man's fate is fixed—why struggle against it?
Koheleth may be reflecting the corollary drawn by the
Greek astrologers that man's career and destiny is determined by his horoscope at the time of birth or (according
to some) at conception.

[100] *i.e.*, fate, which is always stronger than man.

[101] Literally, "many words," but "words" is used by

advantage are they to man? For who knows what is good for a man during the span of his life of vanity? And though he spends [his life] like a shadow,[102] is there any one who can tell man what is to be after him under the sun?[103]

## XV

vii. 1ᵇ-14
*Vanity of
Life.*

The day of death is better than the day of birth.[104]
It is better to go to the house of mourning
than to a house of feasting,
for the former marks the end of all men.[105]

Koheleth also for "things." The thought seems to be that possessions do not make man master of his fate, since wealth has been shown to lead merely to the increase of vanity; it does not enable man to change the course of destiny. Fate is fate—and man has no advantage over anything else in nature, which is all preordained.

[102] *i.e.*, without seeing the reality of things, which to Koheleth means enjoyment.

[103] No one knows what is really good for man, not the wisest nor the incessant worker nor even the astrologer whose knowledge of man's fate does not extend beyond the grave. Koheleth might have added his usual refrain—"therefore, enjoy yourself, though this, too, is vanity and chasing after wind." For a misplaced comment to vi. 12, see below note 123.

[104] In order to counteract the effect of this pessimistic and unorthodox reflection, which runs counter to the accepted belief that life is a blessing from God and that the longer it lasts the greater the blessing, the pious commentator adds at the beginning of the chapter, "Better is a name [*i.e.*, a good reputation] than fine oil," meaning the good name that one leaves behind after life is over. Koheleth is not thinking of this, but only of the vanity of existence—direct and undisguised vanity, not tempered by any consoling thought of immortality or of leaving a fragrant memory behind one. From this point of view, we must approach the chapter which is one of the finest in the book, or we miss its meaning completely.

The mind of the wise is in the house of vii. 4
　　mourning,[106]

but the mind of fools is in the house of mirth,[106]

though this too is vanity.[106a]

Better is the end of a thing than its beginning.[107] vii. 8ª

Do not say, why is it that the former days vii. 10
were better than these, for it is not out of wisdom
that thou puttest this question.[108]　Consider the vii. 13

---

[105] Our pious commentator, still intent upon giving the
reflections of Koheleth a more orthodox and less cynical
turn, adds (2ᵇ-3)

(a) "And the living will take it to mind" and (b) "Dissatisfaction
is better than laughter, for through misfortune the mind is improved."

This point of view is urged by the friends of Job in their
attempts to answer Job's complaint against unjust suffering.

[106] *i.e.*, you may hear sensible talk at a funeral, but
not at a banquet.　A funeral discourse is apt to be better
than an after-dinner speech.　At this point the "maxim"
commentator steps in to introduce some wise saws in illustration of the superiority of wisdom, but what he says takes
us far away from the subject that Koheleth has in mind
(verses 5-6ª, 7, 8ᵇ, and 9).

"It is better to listen to the rebuke of a wise man,
than for a man to listen to the praise [literally, song] of fools."

(6ª) "For as the crackling of thorns under a pot,
so is the applause of fools."

(7) "For extortion deprives a wise man of reason,
and a bribe corrupts the mind."

(8ᵇ) "Better patience than haughtiness."

(9) "Do not be prone to anger,
for anger endures [only] in the bosom of fools."

[106a] *i.e.*, even the discourse of the wise in the house of
mourning is vanity.　There is not much sense even in a funeral
oration, although it is apt to be better than an after-dinner
speech.

[107] This saying *may* likewise be an addition by the
"maxim" commentator.　The "end" is here to be taken
as the outcome or issue.

work of God, for who is able to straighten out what He has made crooked?[109] Therefore, in the day of prosperity, have a good time; and when the day of adversity comes,[110] remember that God has made the one as well as the other, so as to render it impossible for man to find out anything of what is to come hereafter.

## XVI

vii. 15-22
*Vanity of Overright-
eousness and
Overwicked-
ness.*

I have seen all kinds of things in my life of vanity. Here is a righteous man who perishes by his righteousness, and there is a wicked man round-ing out his life[111] in his wickedness. [Therefore] be

[108] Those who laud the past (*laudatores temporis acti*) do not betray their wisdom in imagining that things were better in former days. Things are *always* the same—says Koheleth. Our "maxim" commentator in order again to give a different tone to Koheleth's depressing reflection seizes hold of the term "wisdom" as a handle for some further reflections to emphasize his favorite theme—the advantage of wisdom (verse 11): "Wisdom is better than an inheritance" (so Renan's suggestion by a slight change of the text which says "with" instead of "than") "and an advantage to the living" (lit.: "those who see the sun") (verse 12). "For the protection of wisdom is [as strong] as the protection of silver, and the advantage of knowledge [a variant reads, wisdom] is that it gives life to those who possess it."

[109] Same thought as i. 15. You cannot change matters, and this is another reason against indulging in vain regrets that things are worse at present than they were in the past—even if this were true, which is not the case.

[110] Prosperity and adversity are constantly following each other in endless succession, and no one can tell when the one will come to an end, and the other will set in. Therefore—*carpe diem*, enjoy the present and don't lament when things change. That is the hidden law of nature and God's way of doing things which man cannot fathom.

not overrighteous and be not overwise—why ruin thyself? But do not be overwicked and do not be a fool, why die before thy time?[112] It is good to take vii. 18ª hold of this and not to refrain from that.[113] There vii. 20 is no man on earth so righteous that he [always] does the right thing and never sins.

Furthermore, do not pay attention to all that is said about thee, lest thou hear thy servant defame thee.[114] Surely, many times as thou knowest thou hast defamed others.

## XVII

All this I tested by wisdom. I resolved to be vii. 23-28 wise, but it was far from me. Far off is that which *Vanity of the Search for* exists and very deep—who can find it out?[115] I *Wisdom and for Decent Women.*

---

[111] *i.e.*, has a long life, which according to the conventional view is a sign of God's favor and the reward of virtue, as set forth in Psalms xci. 16; Proverbs x. 27 etc., etc.

[112] If you carry your wickedness *too* far, you will be caught and perish, just like the overrighteous.

[113] Act so as to get the most out of life. Exercise judgment so as to know what to do and what to refrain from doing. The "pious" commentator gives the rather cynical advice a different turn by adding (verse 18ᵇ) "He who fears God will steer clear of everything"—he will neither fall into the pitfalls of wickedness nor suffer because of his righteousness. To this the "wisdom" commentator adds (verse 19): "Wisdom makes a wise man stronger than the ten rulers of a city." The "ten rulers" constitute the city council.

[114] Do not be too anxious to find out what people think of you. You may find out that even the servants of your household gossip about you—just as you gossip about others.

[115] This is probably a popular saying. A similar thought that wisdom is far off is to be found in Job, *e.g.*, xi. 7-8 and xxviii. 12-28.

firmly resolved[116] to search and to seek wisdom. The substance[117] of what I found out was that wickedness is foolish and that folly is madness.

vii. 26ᵃ And I [also] found out that more bitter than death is a woman whose mind is [all] snares and nets, and whose hands are fetters.[118] There is
vii. 28 something [else] which I sought but never found. Among a thousand, I did find a [real] man, but never a [decent] woman among all these.[119]

### XVIII [120]

viii. 2-9 Obey the order of the king.[121]
*The Caprice of Rulers.* Do not be in a hurry to go into his presence,[122]

[116] A gloss to "I resolved" (literally "I turned about") adds "my heart to know," explanatory of the verb used.

[117] A misplaced comment (v. 27ᵃ) to this unusual word "substance" or "sum" explains it as follows, "See this I have found, Koheleth says, one and one to find the sum," *i.e.*, counting up one thing after the other, the total of what can be found out is that wickedness is foolish and does not pay. Surely not much of a result for all one's pains.

[118] Our pious commentator adds (26ᵇ) "He that is good before God shall escape from her, but the sinner shall be caught by her." On Koheleth's attitude toward woman, see above, p. 161 *et seq.*

[119] Our pious commentator adds in characteristic fashion, to furnish the antidote to Koheleth's cynicism (verse 29), "Besides, however, I have found this that God has made man straight, but they have devised many contrivances," *i.e.*, people have found various methods to corrupt the originally fine nature of man.

[120] The section is again full of sayings, added in part by the commentator who is bent upon using every occasion to counterbalance Koheleth's distasteful philosophy by the praise of wisdom, and in part by the pious commentator who seeks to give an orthodox turn to his impious philosophy of

for whatever he desires, he does.                          viii. 4

Inasmuch as the word of a king is supreme,
who can say to him, what art thou doing?[123]

---

life. So the "maxim" commentator introduces the chapter
with (viii. 1)

> (a) "Who is like the wise man, and who knows [as he does] the
> explanation of a matter?"
> (b) "The wisdom of a man illumines his face,
> And the coarseness of his countenance is changed."

(At the beginning of the second verse there is an entirely
meaningless "I"—evidently a textual error.)

[121] A commentator adds "because of the oath of God,"
as though Koheleth wanted to justify obedience to a king
because one has sworn fealty to him. What Koheleth says is
ironically meant. Obey and do what the king says and do
not rush to him with a complaint, for he will in any case do
just as he pleases.

[122] Again the "pious" commentator totally distorts the
irony of the advice—and no doubt with intent—by adding
"Do not plead a bad cause," as though this were the reason
why one should not be in haste to seek an audience of a king.
The entire flavor of the original book is lost by such additions.

[123] The pious commentator (or the "maxim" commentator in a pious spirit) adds (verse 5)

> "The law observer shall know no harm,
> And a wise mind knows the [proper] time and manner."

To this some super-commentator added (verse 6ª,
quoting chapter iii. 1)

> "for to every occurrence there is a time and manner."

The second part of verse 6, reading

> "for man's evil weighs heavily upon him"

is in the style of Koheleth, but is not in place here, as little
as is verse 7,

> "For no one knows the future, so that there might be
> some one to tell him when it will come to pass."

The two utterances (6ᵇ and 7) are perhaps to be taken as
misplaced comments belonging to vi. 12,

> "Who knows what is good for a man's life?"

viii. 8 And yet no one can rule the wind,[124]
or restrain the wind.
No one can lord it over the day of death,
nor ensure escape in war.[125]

All this I experienced by applying my mind
to everything that happened under the sun, where
man has the power to harm his fellow.

### XIX

viii. 10-17
*No Solution
for
Injustice.*

And so [among other things] I have seen
wicked men buried, and [people] coming back
from the sanctified ground,[126] and going about
singing their praises[127] in the very city in which
they acted thus—surely this is vanity.[128]

---

to which some one might appropriately have added "for
man's evil weighs heavily upon him, that there is no one
who knows the future, so that he might tell a man when it
will come." No one can tell, our commentator implies, for no
one knows.

[124] There are limitations even to the powers of a king—
he has no control over the wind, nor over death nor over
the chances of war.

[125] The pious commentator adds (verse 8[b]) "nor will
wickedness help its possessors to escape."

[126] *i.e.*, the cemetery.

[127] *i.e.*, the praises of the wicked. I follow the Greek
text which by the change of a single letter in the Hebrew
obtains a satisfactory meaning, instead of the senseless "are
forgotten." Koheleth's point is that the wicked are not
forgotten, but praised and celebrated even after death, and
in the very place in which they spent their evil lives.

[128] At this point, our pious commentator enters upon an
elaborate argument (verses 11-13) somewhat in the style of
Job's friends to prove that the wicked are punished, even
though the punishment be delayed. "Because the sentence

There is another vanity which happens upon viii. 14 earth—that there are righteous who are treated as though they were wicked, and that there are wicked whose lot is as though they were righteous —I reflected that this is surely vanity.

Therefore, I commend joy, because there is nothing better for a man under the sun than to eat and drink and to be merry, as the accompaniment to his toil during the span of life allotted to him by God under the sun.

When I set my mind to acquire wisdom and viii. 16ª to penetrate to the core of what happens on earth,[129] I realized [finally] in regard to the work of God viii. 17 that man cannot understand what happens under the sun, despite all efforts to seek a solution, and though he deprive himself of sleep day and night,[130] he cannot fathom it; and even if a wise man[131] thinks that he knows—yet he cannot find out.[132] ix. 1ᵈ Man does not know. Everything in the past[133] is vanity.[134]

---

for an evil deed is not promptly carried out, therefore the inclination of man is to do evil [cf. Genesis viii. 21]. But although a sinner does a great deal of evil and is accorded a respite, yet I know that good fortune will attend those who fear God [comment or variant: Those who fear His presence] and that it shall not be well for the wicked, and that he will not lengthen out his days as a shadow [ ? ], because he does not fear the presence of God."

[129] The second part of verse 16 is misplaced. It belongs in the middle of verse 17. See the following note.

[130] This part of the verse "and though .... night" is taken over from v. 16.

[131] *i.e.*, a philosopher.

## XX

ix. 2-10
*Death and
Oblivion the
Common
Fate.
Therefore,
Eat,
Drink, and be
Merry.*

Since there is a common fate to all, to the righteous and to the wicked, to the good [and to the bad],[135] to the clean and to the unclean, to the one who sacrifices and to the one who does not sacrifice; as the virtuous so the sinner, the one who swears and the one who fears an oath—this is the worst evil among all the things that happen under the sun, that there should be one fate to all, and that the mind of the children of men is full of evil and of foolish thoughts while they live and after that—to the dead [they go.]

Yet there is at least some assurance to the one who is classed with the living, for as a living dog, he is better off than a dead lion.[136]  Since the

[132] The greater part of the first verse of chapter ix. is taken up with a comment in the spirit of the pious commentator to give a different turn to Koheleth's thought.  The commentator, repeating from (verse 16) "all this I set my mind to search," says: "all this," namely, that "the righteous and the wise and their works are in the hand of God" to which a super-commentator adds: "also hate and love." After this the original text sets in: "Everything in the past is vanity" (end of section XIX).

[133] Literally: "before them," *i.e.*, anterior to them, *i.e.*, all experience is of no avail in penetrating the mystery about us.

[134] So the Greek text reads instead of the Hebrew "everything."  The difference between "vanity" (*h-b-l*) and "everything" (*h-k-l*) in Hebrew is simply a slight curve to one letter, which changes a Hebrew *b* to *k*.

[135] So the Greek text.

[136] *i.e.*, even though while living he leads a dog's life, that is better than being a dead lion.  So Ehrlich's interpretation, which I follow.  Koheleth here quotes a popular saying, but gives it an ironical turn.

living [at least] know that they will die, whereas the dead know absolutely nothing. Nor is there any remembrance[137] of them, for their memory is forgotten. Aye, their love as their hate and jealousy is utterly lost, and they have no further share forever in all that happens under the sun.

Therefore go, eat thy bread with joy,
And drink thy wine with a merry heart,
For God has already given His approval to
    thy deeds.[138]
At all times be thy garments white,[139]
And let oil not be lacking for thy head.
Enjoy life with the woman of thy love,[140]
All the days of thy vain life,[141]

Which God has given thee under the sun, for that is thy portion in life, and the compensation for thy toil under the sun. Whatever thou canst afford with thy substance do,[142] for there is no activity, or reckoning, or knowledge, and no wisdom in Sheol,[143] whither thou goest.

[137] So by a slight change in the text instead of "reward," which is not in place here.

[138] Namely, by permitting you to be joyful. The same thought as above, note 35.

[139] *i.e.*, clean.

[140] On this passage, for which we have a remarkable parallel in Babylonian literature, see above, p. 174.

[141] A variant or comment that has found its way into the text reads (9[b]): "all the days of thy vanity"—like vii. 15 "my life of vanity."

[142] So correctly interpreted by Ehrlich.

[143] This shows that Koheleth clings to the Semitic belief in a gathering-place in a cave under the earth for all the dead, irrespective of their merits or deeds in this world. The

## XXI

ix. 11-16 And again, I experienced under the sun that
*Chance* The race is not to the swift,
*and the* Nor the battle to the strong;
*Uncertainties*
*of Life.* Wise men lack an income,
Prophets[144] do not possess riches,
And the learned lack wealth, [144a]
But time and chance overtake them all.

Furthermore, man does not know his time.[145] As fish are caught in a net,[146] and as birds are trapped, so the children of men are entrapped at an unlucky moment, when [evil] comes suddenly upon them.

This I experienced[147] under the sun, and it seemed a great [evil][148] to me.

There was a small town with few inhabitants, and a great king came and surrounded it and built great bulwarks against it. And there was in the town a man of humble birth[149] but wise, and he saved the town through his wisdom, but no one took notice

picture that he has in mind of the nether world accords with what we learn from Babylonian literature as a place where the dead lie inactive, conscious but unable to do anything for themselves. See Jastrow, "Hebrews and Babylonian traditions," chapter iv.

[144] So read by a textual change for "men of understanding."

[144a] So by a slight change in the text.

[145] *i.e.*, his end.

[146] The word "evil" added to "net" is superfluous. It belongs perhaps to the close of verse 13, as the subject of the verb "comes suddenly."

[147] The word "wisdom" after "I experienced" is either misplaced, or is an error for "evil" which the context demands, like in ii. 21 and vi. 1.

[148] To be supplied. See preceding note.

of that man of humble birth.[150] And I reflected that  ix. 16
wisdom [nevertheless] is better than strength, even
when the wisdom of the man of humble birth is
despised and his words be not heeded.[151]

## XXII

If a ruler's anger is stirred up against thee,  x. 4-20
do not throw up thy post,[152] for gentleness allays  *Caprice of Rulers.*
real offences.[153]

---

[149] *Misken* "plebeian" as above iv. 13.  See note 64.

[150] This illustration of the lack of reward to those who
merit it probably rests upon some historical incident.

[151] The point is that even though the wise man who
saved the city had not been listened to, nevertheless his
wisdom was superior to mere strength.  Koheleth sets aside
the ingratitude as natural in a topsy-turvy world where all
is chance and uncertainty.  The "maxim" commentator
could not miss such a good opportunity of introducing
some saws about the advantage of wisdom, and so he gives
us a series of six that might just as well have been included in
the Book of Proverbs, for they are entirely in the style of
that collection.  The series extends from ix. 17 to x. 3.

(1) "The words of the wise, though spoken quietly,
    are stronger than the loud cry of an arch-fool."
(2) "Better is wisdom than weapons."

(Here the "pious" commentator adds "one sinner destroys much good"—though this probably belongs before
verse 2 of chapter 10.)

(3) "A dead fly spoils the perfumer's precious oil"
(4) "A little foolishness annuls wisdom."

(The text as it stands gives no sense, but the meaning
appears to be as indicated in the translation, which rests
upon some necessary textual changes.)

(5) "A wise man's mind is on his right side [*i.e.*, the good side],
    but a fool's mind is on the left."
(6) "Also, when a fool struts in his senseless way—
    he says of every one else, 'he is a fool'."

In the text and translation of the third and fourth saying, I
follow Ehrlich.

There is an evil which I observed under the sun, which proceeds from a ruler.

Folly[154] is often placed in high positions, while the choice[155] spirits sit in an humble place.[156]

x. 7 I have seen slaves on horses, and princes walking on foot like slaves.[157]

[152] Do not resign your office, but try to pacify the ruler. The man who resigns confesses his guilt, according to Koheleth who cynically adds that by pacifying a ruler's anger you can escape punishment for *real* offences.

[153] This cynicism is too much for the pious commentator, and so he adds to "great sins," (*i.e.*, real offences,) "as an unintentional error," implying that the "sin" was unintentional, which is exactly what Koheleth did *not* mean to convey. This note, however, has crept into the text in the wrong place. It must be removed from the middle of verse 5 and placed at the end of verse 4.

[154] The abstract is used in the sense of "fools."

[155] Literally: "the tens," *i.e.*, the "upper ten," as we would say. To read "rich," as is commonly done, spoils the thought.

[156] *i.e.*, a ruler often makes bad appointments to offices.

[157] Our maxim commentator again steps in and adds a further series of ten wise saws (verses 8-14[a], 15[a] and 18) which have no connection whatsoever with the thought and philosophy of Koheleth.

(1) "He who digs a pit shall fall therein,
And he who breaks through a wall, a serpent shall bite him."
(2) "He who quarries stones shall be hurt by them,
And he who cleaves wood, shall get a cut."
(3) "If the iron be dull" [comment: *i.e.*, "the edge has not been whetted"] "One must exert one's utmost force."
(4) "The advantage of wisdom is that it secures success."
(5) "If a serpent bites before it is charmed, the charm has no advantage."
(6) "Words from the mouth of a wise man are full of grace, but the lips of the fool confuse him" [*i.e.*, a fool condemns himself by his utterances].
(7) "The beginning of the words issuing from him is folly, and the end of his speech is madness" [a variant says, evil].
(8) "The fool multiplies words."

Woe to thee, O land, whose king is a puppet,     x. 16
and whose princes feast in the morning![158]
Happy art thou, O land, whose king is independent,[159] x. 17
and whose princes feast at the proper time,
for strength and not for guzzling![160]

---

At this point (14[b]) the text has an insertion, "Man does not know what shall be, and who can tell him what will be after him," which has strayed from its proper place—perhaps from chapter vi. 12 or from viii. 7.

(9) "The toil of a fool wears him out."

The balance of this v. 15[b], "Who does not know his way to the city," appears to be a gloss to "fool" in v. 12; 14 or 15.

(10) "Through neglect, the beam-work sinks,
  And through idleness, the house leaks" (verse 18).

The overloading of this chapter through long insertions of sayings and comments, so that only seven verses out of the twenty of which chapter x consists belong to the original text, is particularly noticeable. The aim is unmistakable to change the entire character of the book so as to give it the appearance of a collection of sayings, rather than an exposition of a particular philosophy of life.

[158] A sign of gluttony and riotous living. The proper time for a feast is in the evening, as a recreation after the day's work.

[159] Literally: "a free man," *i.e.*, not at the mercy of his advisers.

[160] Another saying is introduced at this point (verse 18) which belongs to the preceding series—above note 157, and has there been given as 10. Verse 19 is a comment on the closing words of verse 17 "for strength and not for guzzling" to explain that the proper kind of a feast is one arranged "for laughter, with wine to enliven life and sufficient money to provide for everything," *i.e.*, to foot the bill.

The admonition is not quite in the spirit of Koheleth, but also does not contradict that spirit, as do so many of the comments. Even the Psalmist civ. 15 ("Wine that makes a

x. 20 Do not even on thy couch[161] defame a king,
Nor in thy bed-chamber denounce a rich man,
For a bird of heaven will carry the sound,
And a winged creature will reveal the utterance.

### XXIII

xi. 1-6
*The*
*Uncertainty of*
*Things.*
xi. 2

Cast thy bread upon the face of the waters,
for after many days thou shalt find it.[162]
Divide it up into seven or eight portions,[163]
for thou knowest not what[164] will happen on earth.[165]

---

man's spirit merry") approves of drinking, though the general attitude towards viniculture *until* the Exilic period was not favorable. See the author's paper on "Wine in the Pentateuchal Codes" in the *Journal of the American Oriental Society*, vol. xxxiii. pp. 180–192.

[161] By a slight change in the text—suggested by Ehrlich—we obtain "couch" instead of "thought," which forms a better parallel to "bed-chamber."

[162] A bit of shrewd advice to take risks in business by trusting one's goods on ships that will after many days return with a profit, but do not commit all your possessions to *one* venture. Send your goods out in many ships. "Bread" does not refer specifically to corn trade, but is used for "goods" in general.

[163] "Seven or eight" represent a large number. As we say, "Do not put all your eggs in one basket." See Haupt, "The Book of Ecclesiastes" in "Oriental Studies" (Boston, 1899), p. 274, note 52.

[164] A commentator adds the word "evil."

[165] Our "maxim" commentator cannot resist the temptation to add some practical saws of his own (verses 3-4):

(1) "If the clouds be filled with rain,
    they will empty themselves on the earth."
(2) "If a tree falls to the south or to the north,
    where the tree falls, there it remains."
(3) "A wind observer does not sow,
    and a cloud gazer does not harvest."

As thou knowest not the way of the spirit     xi. 5
into the bones in a pregnant womb,[166]
so thou dost not know the work of God who makes
     all things.
In the morning sow thy seed,
and till evening let not thy hand rest,[167]
For thou knowest not which will succeed, this or
     that,
or whether both alike shall be good.

## XXIV

Light is sweet,                      *xi. 7-xii, 8*
And it is pleasant for the eyes to see the sun.    *Enjoy Life*
                                         *while*
Though a man live many years,
Let him be happy throughout.            *You Can,*
And remember the days of darkness,[168]    *before Old*
For they will be many.                 *Age Sets in.*
Whatever is coming[169] is vanity.
Rejoice, O young man in thy youth,      xi. 9[a-b]
And be happy in the days of thy young vigor!
And follow the inclinations of thy mind,

---

The "wind observer" as the "cloud gazer" is the
diviner who looks for omens in winds and clouds. The reference to the diviner is sarcastic. He is an idler who does
not work. This last is more properly an elaboration to verse 6.

While the spirit of these three sayings is quite in
accord with that of Koheleth, yet they take us away from
the immediate theme, and thus reveal their origin as additions by some other hand.

[166] *i.e.,* how life enters into the embryo. So Ehrlich's
explanation.

[167] *i.e.,* be active at all times from youth to old age.

[168] Old age with its infirmities—and death.

[169] *i.e.,* old age and death.

And the sight of thine eyes![170]
xi. 10ᵃ Put away trouble from thy mind,[171]
xii. 1ᵇ Before the evil days come on,
And the years approach of which thou wilt say,
"I have no pleasure in them."
Before the sun is darkened[172] and the clouds return
    after the rain,[173]
The day when the guardians of the house[174] tremble,
And the strong men[175] are bent.
And the grinding maidens cease,[176] for they are few;
And the peering ladies[177] [who look out] through the
    windows grow dim.

---

[170] *i.e.*, do whatever you please to enjoy life. This was too much for our pious commentator, who in order to give an entirely different turn to Koheleth's dangerous advice adds: (9ᶜ) "But know that for all these things God will bring thee into judgment."

[171] Once more the pious commentator adds the antidote and effectively spoils the thought of Koheleth (10ᵇ), "And remove evil from thy flesh, for youth and prime are vanity," and (xii. 1ᵃ) "Remember thy Creator in the days of thy youth."

[172] To which a commentator adds "The light [as well as] the moon and the stars" The "light" is the daylight, while the moon and stars are the lights of night.

[173] The picture of clouds instead of the sun returning after the rain suggests old age which cannot look forward to a renewal of youth and sunshine, but only to inactivity and final darkness.

[174] The hips are meant, or according to the Talmud (Sabbath 152ᵃ) the "ribs."

[175] The legs totter.

[176] The grinding maidens are the teeth which begin to drop out upon the approach of old age.

[177] *i.e.*, the eyes which are pictured as the veiled women of the Orient, peering through lattice windows to see what is going on.

And the doors are closed to the street.[178]
When the sound of the mill is low,[179]
And one rises at the twittering of the birds;[180]
And all the daughters of song lie prostrate.[181]
One is afraid of a height,[182]
And terror is on the road.[183]
And the almond tree blossoms,[184]
And the grasshopper is burdensome,[185]
And the caper berry becomes ineffectual.[186]
Before the silver cord is snapped,[187]

---

[178] According to the Talmud (*ibid.*), this refers to constipation which sets in with old age, but it is more plausible to explain the "closed" doors as the ears, which no longer receive sound.

[179] Loud sounds are only faintly heard when deafness sets in.

[180] Old people are easily awakened and cannot sleep long.

[181] The voice becomes harsh and, later, quite faint.

[182] Climbing is difficult.

[183] Even walking on the highway is fraught with danger when the feebleness of old age sets in.

[184] The blossoms of the almond tree are at first pink at the base but turn white. The reference is to the change of the color of the hair in old age.

[185] According to the Talmud (Sabbath, 152ᵃ), the grasshopper is a picture for the male organ, which would make the line refer to the loss of sexual vitality with the approach of old age. It is also possible, however, that the comparison with the grasshopper is intended to suggest that the smallest weight is a burden, or that a man's frame shrinks, and he loses weight until he seems to be merely a lean grasshopper. Even then life is a burden.

[186] The caper berry was used to excite the sexual passion. With old age sexual pleasures also go.

[187] The spine is bent so that one no longer walks erect.

And the golden bowl is broken.[188]
And the jar is shattered at the spring,
And the wheel is broken at the cistern.[189]
When man goes to his eternal house;
And the wailers go about the street.[190]

xii. 7ª And the dust returns to the earth as it was.[191]

xii. 8ᵇ All is vanity.[192]

xii. 13ª            The End.[193]

---

[188] The golden bowl is the brain, which loses its power when old age sets in.

[189] The jar at the spring may be the picture of the kidneys which refuse to work, and the wheel at the cistern, the machinery of the body—bowels, intestines and liver—which does not carry off the discharges. At all events the two verses together are to indicate that the natural functions are impaired. The whole machinery breaks down. This interpretation of the final utterance of Koheleth as a series of metaphors to describe the failing vitality of all organs and functions with the approach of old age reverts to the early Jewish commentators and exegetes, and is undoubtedly correct. An English physician of the seventeenth century, Dr. John S. Smith, reached the same view independently, and set it forth in his interesting book, "The Portrait of Old Age" (2nd ed. London, 1666).

[190] the hired mourners for the funeral procession, as is still customary in the Orient. These two lines form the last part of verse 5 in the Hebrew text, but their proper place is after verse 6. Through a careless scribe they were misplaced.

[191] Again a direct reference to Genesis iii. 19. The pious commentator, expressing the current orthodox belief, adds "and the spirit returns to God who gave it." That is not Koheleth's view.

[192] This represents the close of the original book. The balance of chapter xii., verses 8-14, is taken up with a series of no less than eleven comments and further endeavors to remove the heterodox taint. First, a commentator or reader added to "all is vanity" a note to complete the summing

up of the teachings of the book (verse 8), "Koheleth says, vanity of vanities." To this another commentator adds a biographical note (verse 9), "And furthermore Koheleth was a wise man [*i.e.*, a philosopher] who in other ways instructed people, by composing and searching." A third hand explains this by asserting that "he compiled many proverbs." Another reader sums up an apologetic view of Koheleth (verse 10) as follows: "Koheleth aimed at a pleasant style [literally, agreeable words] with straightforward expression"; and by way of explanation for the latter phrase, someone added "truthful words," *i.e.*, in order to understand Koheleth, one must bear in mind that his aim was to be perfectly sincere and that, while writing gracefully, he spoke the truth. See further above p. 95. There follows a final insertion in the style of the "maxim" commentator (verse 11):

> "The words of the wise are as goads,
> And collections are as nails, driven with a mace,"

*i.e.*, the aim of sayings is to act as an incentive to man, while collections of such sayings skillfully put together are like nails driven into the proper place. Our "maxim" commentator, in order to justify his interspersion of sayings throughout the book, wants us to look upon the book as *merely* a collection of miscellaneous proverbs strung together in skillful fashion. At the close of the eleventh verse appears an addition "given by one shepherd," which is obscure. "Shepherd" has been taken in the sense of "teacher," and the phrase interpreted to mean that the collection is by one author—so McNeile, "Introduction to Ecclesiastes," p. 24, and Haupt, 1, c., p. 278—but this is hardly satisfactory. The phrase may be simply a comment to "goads," to explain that the word refers to the staff with which a shepherd drives his flock. Then another apologetic commentator has his say by warning us against taking Koheleth too seriously. He indulges in a general fling at the unceasing production of literature (verse 12):

> "Furthermore, beware, my son, of the writing [literally, making] of many books without end,
> And much discussion [?] is a weariness of the flesh."

Last of all, the pious commentator, as his parting shot, in his usual fashion gives expression to the orthodox view (verse 13):
(a) "Fear God, and keep His commandments," to

which a super-commentator adds, (a) "for this [applies to] every man"; and (b) (verse 14), "since for every deed God will bring into judgment," to which again a super-commentator adds (c) "for every hidden act, whether good or bad."

[193] Literally "The end of the matter," *i.e., finis*. This phrase appears at the beginning of verse 13, but ought to have been placed immediately after "all is vanity" (verse 8[b]). As an explanation to the misplaced phrase, someone added "all has been heard"—*i.e.*, the argument is done. These many additions, each independent of the other, bear witness to the interest that the book must have aroused; and it should furthermore be borne in mind, as a further justification for thus regarding verses 9-14 (with the exception of "The end of the matter" at the beginning of verse 13) as a series of miscellaneous comments, that in ancient manuscripts the close of a book is the favorite place for such notes, just as we are inclined to scribble some comment on the last page of a book. Recalling that in ancient days a single manuscript passed through many hands, it will not be surprising to find such comments increasing in number, as time went on. There might easily have been more than eleven such notes.

# *APPENDIX*

# *APPENDIX*

## I

### ADDITIONS BY PIOUS COMMENTATORS, WHOSE AIM IS TO OFFSET THE UNORTHODOX CHARACTER OF THE ORIGINAL BOOK

In i. 13. "Through wisdom," added to conform to the picture of the "wise" Solomon of tradition.

In i. 16. "Wisdom," added to suggest that Solomon's greatness and wealth lay in his surpassing wisdom.

In i. 17. "Wisdom and knowledge," added to "frivolity and foolishness" as the aim proper to the wise king.

In ii. 3. "Though my mind was acting with wisdom," added to suggest that Koheleth, as the disguise for Solomon, did not throw himself senselessly into all kinds of pleasure, but with his mind intent upon noting their effect.

In ii. 9. "However, my wisdom abided with me" is added with the same intent as the addition to ii. 3.

In ii. 12. "Wisdom" added to "madness and folly," to conform to the traditional picture of Solomon.

ii. 26. "For to the man who is good in His sight, He has given wisdom and knowledge and enjoyment, but to the sinner He has assigned the task of gathering and amassing, in order to hand it over to the one who is good in the sight of God"—added to tone down the cynicism in the advice "to eat, drink, and be merry," as the best thing to do with one's life.

In iii. 11. "He [*i.e.*, God] has made everything beautiful in its season," added so as to give a pious turn to Koheleth's pessimistic reflection that the purpose of God is past finding out.

In iii. 14. "God has so made it that men will fear Him" —a pious reflection that interrupts the context.

In iii. 15. "And God seeks out what has been driven away," *i.e.*, nothing worth preserving is lost in this world—a reflection added by the pious commentator.

iii. 17. "But I reflected that God will judge both the righteous and the wicked, for there *is* an appointed time for every occurrence and for every [fixed] act" added to counteract Koheleth's picture of a perverted world in which injustice and wickedness are triumphant, and to give a different turn to the sentiment expressed at the beginning of chapter 3. The superfluous word "fixed" is omitted in the Greek text.

In v. 6. "But fear God," added to give a pious turn to Koheleth's rationalistic view of dreams.

In vii. 1. "Better is a name than fine oil," added to counterbalance Koheleth's unorthodox view that "the day of death is better than the day of birth."

In vii. 2. "And the living will take it to mind," added to give a less objectionable turn to Koheleth's cynicism that it is better to go to a funeral than to a banquet.

vii. 3. "Dissatisfaction is better than laughter, for through misfortune the mind is improved," added with the same intent as the addition to vii. 2.

In vii. 18. "He who fears God will steer clear of everything," added to tone down Koheleth's point of view that one must not be too good or too bad, since excess of either leads one into trouble.

In vii. 26. "He that is good before God shall escape from her, but the sinner shall be caught by her," added to give an assurance of God's protection of the innocent against the wiles of the bad woman.

vii. 29. "Besides, however, I have found this, that God has made man straight, but they have devised many contrivances," added to support the orthodox point of view as found in Genesis, chapter iii, that man's sinful state is due to his disobedience of God's commands.

In viii. 2. "Because of the oath of God," added to Koheleth's advice to "obey the order of a King," to remove the ironical spirit in which it is offered.

In viii. 3. "Do not plead a bad cause," added to convey the impression that this was the reason why Koheleth warns one against rushing into the royal presence.

viii. 5. "The law observer shall know no harm, and a wise mind knows the [proper] time and manner"— an addition obviously in the interest of orthodoxy.

In viii. 8. "Nor will wickedness help its possessors to escape"—an addition that is in the style of the pious commentator, and interrupts Koheleth's point that no one is master of nature or of his fate.

viii. 11-13. "Because the sentence for an evil deed is not promptly carried out, therefore the inclination of man is to do evil, but although a sinner does a great deal of evil and is accorded a respite, yet I know that good fortune will attend those who fear God [comment or variant: Those who fear His presence] and that it shall not be well for the wicked, and that he will not lengthen out his days as a shadow, [?] because he does not fear the presence of God"—a long addition to counteract the cynicism of Koheleth, who has just said that the wicked flourish and are even honored after they have passed away.

In ix. 1. "That the righteous and the wise and their works are in the hand of God," added to indicate what Koheleth meant by "All this," which he was determined to find out. A super-commentator adds "also hate and love" *sc.* are in the hands of God. See further the comment to this verse.

In ix. 18. "One sinner destroys much good," added as a "pious" maxim and perhaps misplaced. It fits in better at x. 2.

In x. 5. "As an unintentional error," added to "real offences," to tone down the cynicism involved in Koheleth's statement.

In xi. 9. "But know that for all these things God will bring thee into judgment"—added as the antidote to the advice to enjoy oneself to the full.

In xi. 10—xii. 1. Three insertions: (a) "And remove evil from thy flesh," added to counterbalance "And put away trouble from thy mind," (b) for youth and prime are vanity, and (c) "Remember thy Creator in the days of thy youth," added to further counter-act the objectionable character of Koheleth's advice to the young.

In xii. 7. "And the spirit returns to God who gave it" —added to make Koheleth conform to the current orthodox belief.

xii. 12. "Beware, my son, of the writing of many books without end, and much discussion [?] is a weariness to the flesh," added as a warning not to take Koheleth too seriously, in case the pious additions fail of their intended purpose to change the objectionable tone and general unorthodox character of the book in its original form.

In xii. 13. "Fear God and keep His commandments, for this [applies to] every man," added as a final summary.

xii. 14. "Since for every deed God will bring into judgment," added as a parting shot against the cynicism and skepticism of Koheleth. A super-commentator supplemented this by adding "for every hidden act, whether good or bad."

# *APPENDIX*

## II

PROVERBS AND PROVERBIAL SAYINGS, INTER-
SPERSED THROUGHOUT THE BOOK OF
KOHELETH, AND WHICH LIKEWISE REPRE-
SENT ADDITIONS TO THE ORIGINAL WORK,
MADE IN ORDER TO CONVEY THE IMPRES-
SION THAT THE BOOK OF KOHELETH IS
*MERELY* A COLLECTION OF WISE AND PRAC-
TICAL SAYINGS LIKE THE BOOK OF PROV-
ERBS. IT WAS ALSO HOPED THAT BY THUS
OVERLOADING THE BOOK WITH UNOBJEC-
TIONABLE MAXIMS, THE CYNICAL SAY-
INGS, INTRODUCED BY KOHELETH HIM-
SELF IN HIS BOOK, WOULD BE COUNTER-
BALANCED.

i. 15. "The crooked cannot be straightened,
And the lacking cannot be supplied."

1. 18. "For in much wisdom is much trouble,
And increase of knowledge is increase of pain."

In ii. 14. "The wise man has his eyes in his head,
But the fool walks in darkness."

iii. 3-8. "There is a time to destroy, and a time to repair.
A time to break down, and a time to
build up.
A time to weep, and a time to laugh.
A time to mourn, and a time to dance.
A time to scatter stones, and a time to
gather stones.
A time to embrace, and a time to refrain
from embracing.
A time to seek, and a time to give up as lost.
A time to keep, and a time to throw away.
A time to rip, and a time to sew.
A time to keep silent, and a time to speak.
A time to love, and a time to hate.
A time of war, and a time of peace."

iv. 5.  "The fool folds his hands and consumes his own flesh."

iv. 9-12.  "Two are better than one,
　　for they secure a better return for their toil."
"In case they fall, the one can lift his fellow up, but if a single person falls, there is none to lift him up."
(This may be an explanatory comment to the saying about "two being better than one," giving the reason therefor.)
　　"If two sleep together, they keep warm,
　　　　but how can a single person keep warm?
　　　　And if some one attacks, there are two to withstand;
　　　　and a triple cord is not easily snapped."

In v. 14.  "As he came naked from his mother's womb, so he returns as he came."

vi. 7.  "All the toil of a man is for his mouth,
　　and yet the appetite is never satisfied."

vii. 5-6ᵃ.  "It is better to listen to the rebuke of a wise man,
　　than for a man to listen to the praise of fools."
"For as the crackling of thorns under a pot,
　　so is the applause of fools."

vii. 7.  "Extortion deprives a wise man of reason,
　　and a bribe corrupts the mind."

In vii. 8.  "Better patience than haughtiness."

vii. 9.  "Do not be prone to anger,
　　for anger endures [only] in the bosom of fools."

vii. 11.  "Wisdom is better than an inheritance,
　　and an advantage to the living."

vii. 12.  "For the protection of wisdom is [as strong] as the protection of silver,
And the advantage of knowledge [variant, wisdom] is that it gives life to those who possess it."

vii. 19.  "Wisdom makes a wise man stronger than the ten rulers of a city."

# APPENDIX

viii. 1.  "Who is like the wise man, and who knows
[as he does] the explanation of a matter?"
"The wisdom of a man illumines his face,
And the coarseness of his countenance is changed."
ix. 17-x, 3.  "The words of the wise, though spoken
quietly, are stronger than the loud cry of an arch-
fool."
"Better is wisdom than weapons."
"A dead fly spoils the perfumer's precious oil."
"A little foolishness annuls wisdom."
"A wise man's mind is on his right side,
but a fool's mind is on his left."
"Also, when a fool struts in his senseless way,
he says of everyone else, 'he is a fool.' "
x. 8-15².  "He who digs a pit shall fall therein,
And he who breaks through a wall, a serpent shall bite him."
"He who quarries stones shall be hurt by
them,
And he who cleaves wood shall get a cut."
"If the iron be dull [which a commentator
explains as meaning, 'the edge has
not been whetted'], one must exert
one's utmost force."
"The advantage of wisdom is that it secures
success."
"If a serpent bites before it is charmed,
the charm has no advantage."
"Words from the mouth of a wise man are
full of grace,
but the lips of the fool confuse him."
"The beginning of the words issuing from
him [i.e., from a fool] is folly,
And the end of his speech is madness"
[variant, evil].
"The fool multiplies words."
"The toil of a fool wears him out."

251

x. 18. "Through neglect, the beamwork sinks,
  And through idleness, the house leaks."
xi. 3-4. "If the clouds be filled with rain,
  they will empty themselves on the earth."
 "If a tree falls to the south or to the north,
  where the tree falls, there it remains."
 "A wind observer does not sow,
  And a cloud gazer does not harvest."
xii. 11. " The words of the wise are as goads,
  And collections are as nails, driven with a
  mace."

### III
### MISCELLANEOUS COMMENTS AND GLOSSES ADDED TO THE BOOK

i. 1. The heading, added subsequently to the completion of the book, read originally (on the basis of i. 12)
"Words of Koheleth, a King in Jerusalem," to which someone added "son of David," to confirm the implication that Koheleth is Solomon. See further, page 65, *et seq.*

i. 2. "Vanity of Vanities, says Koheleth, Vanity of Vanities, All is vanity."—A summary, taken over from the end of the book, xii. 8.

In i. 5. The word "rises" toward the end of the verse is to be taken as an explanation of the preceding word.

In ii. 6. "of trees"—added to "forest" by way of explanation.

In iii. 12. "to do good," probably intentionally changed from "to look upon good," *i.e.*, to have a good time.

In iii. 17. "fixed," misplaced comment, belonging to "act."

In iii. 18. "they to them"—probably misplaced gloss, belonging to v. 19. See the comment in note 50 to v. 18.

# APPENDIX

In iii. 21.  "to the earth," explanatory gloss to "goes down."

In iv. 15.  "the second" added to "child," and probably a misplaced note to "the one" in v. 10.

In iv. 16.  "before whom he was," added as a note to the word "all."

In v. 3.  "For He (*i.e.*, God) has no pleasure in fools," a misplaced gloss to the word "fools" in iv. 17.

In v. 8.  "attached to a field" (translation doubtful!) appears to be a misplaced and corrupt gloss to the word "laborer" in v. 11.

In v. 12.  "to his hurt," added as an explanatory gloss to "owner."

In vi. 3.  "And he has not even a burial," added to complete the picture of an unhappy and useless life, because deprived of joy.

In vii. 12.  "wisdom," added as a variant to "knowledge," to suggest the synonymity of the two terms.

In vii. 25.  "my heart to know," gloss explanatory of the phrase, "I resolved."

vii. 27.  "See, this, I have found, Koheleth says, one and one to find the sum," a comment to explain the word "substance," in verse 25.

viii. 6-7.  Two insertions: (a) "for to every occurence there is a time and manner," added by a super-commentator to the "pious" reflection in v. 5; (b) "for man's evil weighs heavily upon him that there is no one who knows the future, so that he might tell a man when it will come"—likewise a misplaced comment and belonging probably to vi. 12.

In viii. 12.  "Those who fear His presence," a variant or comment to "those who fear God."

In ix. 1.  "Also hate and love," added by a super-commentator.

In ix. 9.  "All the days of thy vanity," a variant or comment to "all the days of thy vain life."

In ix. 12. "evil," added to "net" is quite superfluous. The word "evil" may be misplaced, and have been intended as the subject of "comes suddenly" in v. 13.

In x. 10. "the edge has not been whetted," added as an explanatory note to "if the iron be dull."

In x. 13. "evil," added as a variant to "madness."

In x. 14. "Man does not know what shall be, and who can tell him what will be after him"—probably a misplaced comment. It fits in at vi. 12 or viii. 7.

In x. 15. "Who does not know his way to the city"— a gloss to the word "fool" in v. 12, 14 or 15.

x. 19. "A feast is made for laughter,
with wine to enliven life,
and sufficient money to provide for everything"
—added as an explanation to the proper kind of feasting.

In xi. 2. "evil," added to "what" by some commentator.

In xii. 2. "And the light and the moon and the stars," added by way of elaboration and as a comment to "sun," to suggest that by "sun" all phases of light are meant—the light of the moon and of the stars as well.

In xii. 8. "Vanity of vanities, says Koheleth," added to "all is vanity," which was originally the close of the book.

For the eleven comments at the end of the book xii. 9-14, see note 192 to the translation, p. 240. Of these, three (xii. 12-14) are by the "pious" commentator, (see above, p. 248), with an addition by a supercommentator "for every hidden act, whether good or bad" (xii. 14$^b$), one (xii. 11) by the "maxim" commentator (above p. 241), and the balance represent miscellaneous comments partly of an explanatory and partly of an apologetic character.

## APPENDIX

Purely explanatory is the comment to the words, "End of the matter" (verse 13ᵃ), *i.e.*, *finis*, the end of the book, to which the comment "all has been heard," *i.e.*, the argument is finished, has been added. Verses 9-10 contain five comments of an apologetic nature, one superimposed on the other in succession, to explain who Koheleth was, what he did and what his aim was, *viz.*, (a) he was wise, and taught people, (b) he compiled many proverbs, (c) he tried to write in an interesting manner, (d) but he was frank, (e) he spoke the truth. Quite obscure is the comment, "given by one shepherd" (in v. 11). It may be a misplaced comment to the word "goads" in the first part of verse 11.